Campbell Curricul

Orton-Gillingham Word List Dictionary

Volume 2:

Digraphs, Trigraphs

One-Syllable Open Vowel

VCE, Vowel Teams

Sounds of Y

Compound Words

by Valerie Arredondo, M.A.T

Orton-Gillingham Word List Dictionary Series

Volume 1	Volume 2	Volume 3
Consonants	Digraphs & Trigraphs	Soft C & G
Short Vowels	One-Syllable Open Vowel	R-Controlled
FLOSS	VCE (silent E)	W-Controlled
Blends	Vowel Teams	-CLE (Simple Syllables)
End Blends	Sounds of Y	Silent Letters
Closed Syllable Exceptions	Multiple Spellings	Complex Letter Teams
Compound Words	Compound Words	Simple Suffixes
		Compound Words
		Due for release early 2020

Future Volumes will include: Prefixes, Advanced Suffixes, Anglo-Saxon, Greek, and Latin Roots, Multi-Syllable Words, Syllable Rules, Syllable Division, Word Families, and Red Words.

I hope you will find this book to be an invaluable addition to your professional resources. Please consider giving this volume a 5-star Amazon review. We are a small family business and your reviews will help other educators to choose the best books for their continuing professional growth & development.

Short Table of Contents

Letter Team Quick Index (Alphabetical)

Extended Table of Contents

Extended Table of Contents

Vowels & Vowel Teams

One Syllable Open Vowel

VCE

VE

Extended Table of Contents

Vowels & Vowel Teams, continued

EA & OA

OO

I/Y Alternates

Extended Table of Contents

Vowels & Vowel Teams, continued

U/W Alternates

Sounds of Y

Extended Table of Contents

Resources

Ideas for Using this Book

❖ The lists in this series are designed to be used by any Orton-Gillingham based instructor or teacher. It does not matter what order or program you are using.

❖ Design your lessons easily by looking up any letter or letter team. The **Table of Contents** makes it easy find whatever you need.

❖ The **LT's** (Letter Teams) column is a list of all the additional letters and letter teams in the word. (In this book phonograms/phonemes/graphemes are often referred to as letters or letter teams. I also use the term phonogram frequently because it combines the phoneme and grapheme aspects of each letter or letter team).

❖ The **LT's** column can help you choose fair words. In the list below (for the blend **BL**), you can see that the word **blab** has no other letter teams besides **BL**. The word **black** has **CK**, the word blade has **A-E**, and the word Blair has **AI**. This makes it easy to look at the list and quickly choose the words that would be fair words for your student.

Base	LT's	-s/-es	-ed	-ing	-y/-ly	-er	-est
blab		blabs	blabbed	blabbing		blabber	
black	ck	blacks	blacked			blacker	blackest
blade	a-e	blades					
Blair	ai						
Blake	a-e						
blame	a-e	blames	blamed	blaming		blamer	

❖ Use the Letter Team **(LT's)** column to find words that reinforce recently learned concepts. In the list below **(-NK)**, if your student needed more practice with **R-blends**, you could look in the Letter Team column to find **-NK** words that also have **R-Blends**. (**brink, drink**)

Base	LT's	-s/-es	-ed	-ing	-y/-ly	-er	-est
blink	bl	blinks	blinked	blinking		blinker	
brink	br						
chink	ch	chinks	chinked	chinking			
clink	cl	clinks	clinked	clinking			
drink	dr	drinks		drinking		drinker	
ink		inks	inked	inking			

❖ Keep this book handy during lessons, in case your student needs extra practice with a specific letter team.

❖ Use the details and rules listed under each letter team to fully understand how that letter team is used in the English language. Below is an example of some of the details in the **FLOSS** section:

- **SS** follows the **FLOSS** rule. **F, L, S,** and **Z** are usually doubled at the end of a one-syllable short-vowel word. There are some exceptions to this rule.
- The double **SS** indicates that the word ending in **S** is not plural.
- Words that end in **SS** indicate a plural by adding **-ES,** instead of **-S** (**bless - blesses**).

❖ Use the word lists and letter teams **(LT's)** columns to make review lesson for students. If you are using a structured curriculum, sometimes the curriculum will proceed too quickly for a particular student. These lists make it easy to create review lessons.

❖ Use the letter teams **(LT's)** columns to find fair words. You can eliminate words that have phonograms your students have not learned yet.

❖ Use word lists to find theme and content related words that have letter teams your students have already learned.

❖ Practice reading and spelling words with suffixes. Each list includes a column for the suffixes **-s, -es, 's, -ed, -ing, -y, -ly, -er/-ar/-or** and **-est**. (For names that have apostrophe **'S** for a name **(Jack's)**, the apostrophe **'S** indicates possession and not the plural form of a word).

Base	-s/-es/'s	-ed	-ing	-y/-ly	-er/-ar/-or	-est
fun				funny	funnier	funniest
gum	gums	gummed	gumming	gummy	gummier	gummiest

❖ Print out individual phonogram cards for each student. You can print the cards on paper, or card stock. Cards can be laminated, as well. Send an extra set of cards home for practice.

❖ Give your students their own phonogram cards so they can draw key word pictures on the cards.

❖ Make word sorts, based on different phonograms.

❖ Help your students make word sums with the Word Sums template.

❖ Print the Letter and Phonogram Tiles (from the Resource section) onto paper or tagboard to make affordable manipulatives for Word Building activities.

st ing

b a t

❖ Make games with the Go Fish Cards and Blank Card templates. These games work best if they are printed on thick tagboard, so that they are not see-through. You can also use the phonogram cards and spelling tiles cards to make games.

❖ Use the Resources List to find books that are informative about dyslexia, phonics, and word study.

❖ See Volume 1 for specific examples of ways to use this book.

How to Read the Entries

Headers – At the top of each word list page is a header. If that particular letter/letter team has more than one sound, a sample word will be given below the header to indicate which sound applies to that list. For **OW** there are two sounds, **/oh/** in **snow** and **/ow/** in **cow**, and therefore there are two different word lists.

OW

snow

OW

cow

Each letter or letter team (phonogram) has information at the top of the page that tells you about that letter team. Below is an example of an entry. On the following page is explanation of what each detail means.

OW

/ō/ in snow

Position: End

Vocalization: Voiced

Classification: Vowel Digraph

Group: Vowel Team, U/W Alternate

Multiple spellings (common) /ō/: O, O-E, OA, <u>OW</u>

Multiple spellings (rare) /ō/: OE, OU

Multiple sounds for OW: /ow/ in cow, <u>/ō/ in snow</u>

/ō/ in snow – The first listing is a pronunciation guide. Pronunciation varies widely by dialect.

Position: This tells you if the phonogram is found more frequently at the beginning, middle, or end of a word. In general, consonant letter teams are found at the beginning and end of a root word, and vowels are found in the middle, but this does vary for some words.

Students should learn that the positions of each letter team apply to the root word only. Once prefixes or suffixes are added, a letter team that is commonly found at the end of a root word – like **OY (toy, ploy),** may end up appearing to be in the middle of a word **(toying, employer).**

Vocalization: Sounds are considered voiced or unvoiced. Voiced sounds are made in the throat/larynx. Unvoiced sounds are made only with the mouth. Unvoiced does not mean silent.

All vowels are voiced, so if there is a spoken vowel in a letter team, it will be voiced. If there is a combination of sounds in a letter team and at least one of the sounds is voiced, it will be categorized as voiced. Most letter sounds are voiced. Unvoiced letters/teams include **f, p, s, h, t, k, th, sh,** and **ch.**

Many voiced letters and letter teams have a corresponding unvoiced sound that is made with the same shape of the mouth. For example, **/v/** and **/f/** are made in the same mouth shape with the bottom lip touching the top teeth, but **/v/** is voiced and **/f/** is unvoiced. These double sounds are more likely to confuse students when they are listening and reading.

Classification: Classification is the more formal linguistic word for the letter or letter team. It tells the function of the team. For example, **SH** is a digraph. That means that two letters come together to form one sound.

Group: Group is similar to classification, but terms listed are more informal words or phrases that many educators use when teaching children. For example, **SH, TH** and **CH** are often called the "H-Brothers" by OG practitioners and teachers as an easy way to group the **H**-digraphs together.

Multiple spellings (common) and Multiple spellings (rare) Multiple spellings are different ways to spell the same sound. The **/ō/** sound in **snow** can also be spelled **O, O-E, OA, OW**, or **OU.**

Letter teams are listed in order of how common they are, with the most common being listed first and the least common being listed last. Common multiple spellings have over 50 root words that use that spelling **(O, O-E, OA, OW)** and rare multiple spellings have under 50 words each **(OE, OU).** Of course, it would make more sense to teach children the most common spellings first, because they will apply to the highest number of words. The spelling that applies to each word list is underlined, so you can quickly see how common that spelling is compared to other spellings.

See the multiple spellings charts in the resource section for more information.

Multiple sounds: Just as there are multiple spellings for each sound, there are multiple sounds for each spelling. In the example above, **OW** can say /ow/ in **cow** or /ō/ in **snow**. In this book, each sound has its own separate list.

Details: Each letter or letter team (phonogram) has a bullet point list of special details that apply to that team. For example, below is the beginning of the detail list for **CH**:

- **CH** has three different sounds. **CH** says **/ch/** in **chair** in most English words, **/k/** in words of Greek origin, like **chord**, and **/sh/** in words of French origin, like **charade**.
- See the **NCH** and **TCH** lists in the End Digraphs section for more words with **CH**.
- Words that end in **/ch/** change to a plural by adding **-ES,** instead of **-S (porch – porches, reach - reaches).**

<u>Helpful Tips</u>

- Words, sounds, letters, and letter teams are in **bold** print. Sounds are indicated by slash marks **/sh/** in **ship.**

- Compound words are included as a separate list below each letter team's word list.

- Words listed with italics in the base word column have an unusual or irregular spelling or pronunciation. Some of those pronunciations will become clearer once the students work with morphology, multisyllable words and affixes. A * next to a letter team in the LT's column indicates which spelling/sound is unusual. Words with two stars ** have special notes that are located below the word list. Words listed in the **-er** and **-est** columns that are in italics are words that were formed from the **-y** form of the word (**hair/hairy/hairier/hairiest**). These italicized words were not formed from the base word that is listed at the beginning of the row.

- The focus of this book is on phonograms. Multi-syllable words are only provided for concepts that have very few single-syllable words. For multi-syllable words in this volume, the **LT's** column will list phonograms, such as **PR** in **preheat**, instead of affixes like **PRE-**. Future volumes will cover prefixes, suffixes, and mutli-syllable words.

- Volumes 1-3 in this series are designed to be one-syllable and compound words for the beginning learner. Future volumes in this series will cover multi-syllable words. Multi-syllable words are provided in this volume only if the number of single-syllable words is limited. Multi-syllable words are likely to have schwa sounds and other tricky pronunciations, which are better suited to a more advanced student.

- Many educators use the terms root word and base word interchangeably, and they may have different meanings for each term. In this series, the term **Root Word** refers to the most basic version of a word, which has no prefixes or suffixes added to it **(pack, run).** The term **Base Word** refers to a word that may already have affixes attached, but it can still have more affixes added. For example, the word **packing** already has **-ING** added to **pack.** The word **packing** serves as a base word for the word **repacking.** So, the word **packing** could be referred to as the **Base Word,** but not the **Root Word**. Some words in the base words column already have affixes attached to them, and therefore many of these words are not pure roots. That is why they are called base words and not root words.

- Names in this book include their apostrophe form in the s/es/'s column. Please note that apostrophe **'S** is not the plural of a name. It indicates possession. The word "Pat's" mean's something belongs to Pat. The word "Pats" indicates that there are more than one person named Pat.

- In general, I only use the hyphen in front of suffixes **(-ING, -EST).** However, I occasionally use a hyphen in front of a letter team that only falls at the end of a word because there needs to be a clarification about that specific letter team. For example, I put a hyphen in front of the letter team **-YE** to distinguish it from the word **YE** as in "ye old shoppe".

- In compound words, two letters next to each other may appear to be a digraph, but they are in fact letters from two separate words. u**p** + **h**ill = u**ph**ill (not digraph **PH**), an**t** + **h**ill = an**th**ill (not digraph **TH**). Every attempt has been made to ensure that the compound words in these lists have only true phonemes.

- Regional dialects should always be considered when teaching children. You may come across a phoneme/sound that seems to be different from how you pronounce it in your area. For example, in some areas, short **O** and **AW** have the same sound (/ah/). In other areas, they have two different sounds /ah/ and /a-w/. Another example: The sound for short **E** can be completely different sound in one part of the country than it is another part of the country.   Sounds also differ widely between English speaking countries. Teachers will need to adjust the phonemes/sounds in this book to reflect their local speech sounds, and may also need to adjust to the speech sounds of children who have moved into the area from other dialects and children who have a first language that is not English.

- The details for each letter team are sometimes extensive. It would be unrealistic for children to learn every one of these details. Some of the details will be helpful for the children to learn, and some of the details will be primarily helpful for the educator to better understand the English language and what they are teaching. Details can also be helpful when children have questions about specific words.

- In reference to the phrase "**B says /b/**," some linguists insist that we should never communicate to our students that letters "say" a sound, because "letters don't talk", and also because multiple sounds (phonemes) can be attached to single letters and letter teams (graphemes). However, I believe that using the word "say", such as "**B says /b/**" is the easiest way to communicate to children that there is a transition between print and sound. In fact, recent research has found that the translation of print into auditory sound & auditory memory is how children best retain and recall words (orthographic mapping).

It also makes more sense when working with children to simply say "**B** says **/b/**" than to say something like, "The grapheme **B** expresses itself with the phoneme **/b/**." As far as multiple sounds for each letter, children easily understand that a letter can "say" more than one sound. Therefore, I happily use the word "say" in this volume, and readers can of course do whatever seems best to them.

Multiple Spellings and Sounds

Multiple spelling lists are found both in the charts in the resource section, and in the details section for each letter or letter team.

- Multiple spellings are divided into common and rare spellings, and then listed in descending order (most common spelling first to least common spelling last).*

- Spellings that are labeled **common** have more than 50 words, and spellings that are labeled **rare** have fewer than 50 words. In general, there is a very big difference between common and rare spellings, with most common spellings ranging in the 100-2000 word range, and with rare spellings mostly having fewer than 30 words. It would make sense, of course, to teach the common spellings first, since that includes the largest bulk of words that children will read.

- Here is an example. In the list below, A is the most common spelling for the sound/phoneme /ā/, and **AE** is the least common spelling.

    Multiple spellings (common) /ā/: A, A-E, AI, AY

    Multiple spellings (rare) /ā/: EI, EY, EA, EIGH, AE

- Multiple sounds for each letter team are also listed in the detail section of that spelling.

    Multiple sounds for AE: /ā/ in bae and /ē/ in algae

*I was able to list these phonograms in order of use, due in great thanks to the following people and resources: Margaret Bishop & Paul Hanna for their word counts, Neil Ramsden for his word search program (neilramsden.co.uk>spelling>searcher), Rome & Osman (2004) for their multiple spellings cards, and the Merriam-Webster Dictionary.

H-Digraph
Printable Cards

ch	sh
th	wh

gh	ph
rh	

ch

/ch/ in chess

Position: Beginning and End

Vocalization: Unvoiced

Classification: Digraph

Group: H-Brothers

Multiple spellings (common) /ch/: <u>CH</u>, TCH

Multiple sounds for CH: <u>/ch/ in chess</u>, /k/ in choir, /sh/ in chute

- **CH** has three different sounds. **CH** says **/ch/** in **chair** in most English words. It also says **/k/** in words of Greek origin, like **chord**, and **/sh/** in words of French origin, like **charade**.
- See the **NCH** and **TCH** lists in the End Digraphs section for more words with **CH**.
- Words that end in **/ch/** change to a plural by adding **-ES**, instead of **-S (porch – porches, reach - reaches).**
- **T** could be considered a multiple spelling for **CH**. Many words that start with the letters **TR** are pronounced **CHR (train, track)**, and words with **T** in front of a **U** suffix are often pronounced **CH (actual, texture).** **T** is not included here as an official multiple spelling, because most **OG**-based programs do not include it, however, it's good for children to be aware that some words with **/ch/** sounds may be spelled with a **T**. **OG** programs often introduce the **T** as **/ch/** when they get to multi-syllable words, connectives, or suffixes.

See next page for word lists.

ch

chess

Beginning

Base	LT's	-s/-es	-ed	-ing	-y/-ly	-er	-est
Chad		Chad's					
chaff	ff	chaffs					
chain	ai	chains	chained	chaining			
chair	air	chairs					
chalk	alk	chalks	chalked	chalking			
champ	mp	champs					
Chance	c(e)	Chance's					
Chang	ang	Chang's					
change	ang g(e)	changes	changed	changing		changer	
chant	nt	chants	chanted	chanting		chanter	
chap		chaps	chapped	chapping			
chard	ar						
charge	ar -ge	charges	charged	charging		charger	
Charles	ar -es	Charles'					
charm	ar	charms	charmed	charming		charmer	
chart	ar	charts	charted	charting		charter	
chase	a-e	chases	chased	chasing		chaser	
Chase	a-e	Chase's					
chat		chats	chatted	chatting	chatty	chatter	
cheap	ea				cheaply	cheaper	cheapest
cheat	ea	cheats	cheated	cheating		cheater	
check	ck	checks	checked	checking		checker	
cheek	ee	cheeks			cheeky	*cheekier*	*cheekiest*
cheep	ee	cheeps	cheeped	cheeping			
cheer	eer	cheers	cheered	cheering			
chess	ss						
chest	st	chests					
chew	ew	chews	chewed	chewing	chewy	*chewier*	*chewiest*
chick	ck	chicks					
chide	i-e	chides	chided	chiding			
chief	ie	chiefs			chiefly		
child	ild						
chill	ll	chills	chilled	chilling	chilly	*chillier*	*chilliest*
chime	i-e	chimes	chimed	chiming			
chimp	mp	chimps					
chin		chins	chinned	chinning			
chink	ink	chinks	chinked	chinking			
chip		chips	chipped	chipping		chipper	

Beginning, continued

Base	LT's	-s/-es	-ed	-ing	-y/-ly	-er	-est
Chip		Chip's					
chirp	ir	chirps	chirped	chirping	chirpy	*chirpier*	*chirpiest*
chive	i-e	chives					
chock	ck						
choice	oi c(e)	choices					choicest
chomp	mp	chomps	chomped	chomping			
chop		chops	chopped	chopping	choppy	*choppier*	*choppiest*
chore	ore	chores					
chow	ow	chows	chowed	chowing			
chuck	ck	chucks	chucked	chucking			
Chuck	ck	Chuck's					
chug		chugs	chugged	chugging			
chum		chums			chummy	*chummier*	*chummiest*
chunk	unk	chunks	chunked	chunking	chunky	*chunkier*	*chunkiest*
church	ur	churches	churched				
churn	ur	churns	churned	churning			

End

Base	LT's	-s/-es	-ed	-ing	-y/-ly	-er	-est
beach	ea	beaches	beached	beaching	beachy	*beachier*	*beachiest*
belch		belches	belched	belching		belcher	
birch	ir	birches					
bleach	bl ea	bleaches	bleached	bleaching		bleacher	
breach	br ea	breaches	breached	breaching			
broach	br oa	broaches	broached	broaching			
coach	oa	coaches	coached	coaching			
couch	ou	couches	couched	couching			
crouch	cr ou	crouches	crouched	crouching			
each	ea						
gulch		gulches					
larch	ar	larches					
leech	ee	leeches	leeched	leeching			
lurch	ur	lurches	lurched	lurching			
march	ar	marches	marched	marching		marcher	
March	ar						
much							

ch

chess

End, continued

Base	LT's	-s/-es	-ed	-ing	-y/-ly	-er	-est
mulch		mulches	mulched	mulching		mulcher	
ouch	ou						
parch	ar	parches	parched	parching			
peach	ea	peaches			peachy	*peachier*	*peachiest*
perch	er	perches	perched	perching			
poach	oa	poaches	poached	poaching		poacher	
pooch	oo	pooches					
porch	or	porches					
preach	pr ea	preaches	preached	preaching	preachy		
reach	ea	reaches	reached	reaching			
rich		riches			richly	richer	richest
roach	oa	roaches					
scorch	sc or	scorches	scorched	scorching		scorcher	
slouch	sl ou	slouches	slouched	slouching		scorcher	
starch	st ar	starches	starched	starching	starchy	*starchier*	*starchiest*
such							
teach	ea	teaches		teaching		teacher	
torch	or	torches	torched	torching			
vouch	ou	vouches	vouched	vouching		voucher	
which	wh						
zilch							

Compound

Base	LT's	-s/-es	-ed	-ing
archduke	ar u-e	archdukes		
archway	ar ay	archways		
armchair	ar air	armchairs		
beachfront	ea fr nt	beachfronts		
brainchild	br ai -ild			
chainsaw	ai aw	chainsaws		
chairlift	air ft	chairlifts		
chalkboard	alk oar	chalkboards		
checkbook	ck oo	checkbooks		
checklist	ck st	checklists		
checkpoint	ck oi nt	checkpoints		
checkup	ck	checkups		
cheekbone	ee o-e	cheekbones		

chess

Compound, continued

Base	LT's	-s/-es	-ed	-ing
cheesecake	ee -se a-e	cheesecakes		
chessboard	ss oar	chessboards		
chickpea	ck ea	chickpeas		
childbirth	ild ir th			
childcare	ild are			
childproof	ild pr oo			
chinstrap	str	chinstraps		
chipboard	oar	chipboards		
chopstick	st ck	chopsticks		
cornstarch	or st ar			
crosscheck	cr ss ck	crosschecks	crosschecked	crosschecking
deckchair	ck air	deckchairs		
godchild	ild			
grandchild	gr nd ild			
headcheese	ea ee -se			
highchair	igh air	highchairs		
outreach	ou ea	outreaches		
overreach	er ea	overreaches		
parchment	ar nt	parchments		
paycheck	ay ck	paychecks		
pushchair	u sh air	pushchairs		
stepchild	ild st			
torchlight	or ight	torchlights		
touchdown	ou ow	touchdowns		
vouchsafe	ou a-e	vouchsafes	vouchsafed	vouchsafing
wheelchair	wh ee air	wheelchairs		
whichever	wh er			
woodchuck	oo ck	woodchucks		

ch

/k/ in choir

Position: Beginning and End

Vocalization: Unvoiced

Classification: Digraph

Group: H-Brothers

Multiple spellings (common) /k/: C, K, CK, <u>CH</u>

Multiple spellings (rare) /k/: QUE

Multiple sounds for CH: /ch/ in chess, <u>/k/ in choir</u>, /sh/ in chute

- **CH** has three different sounds. **CH** says **/ch/** in **chess** in most English words. It also says **/k/** in words of Greek origin, like **chord**, and **/sh/** in words of French origin, like **charade**.
- **CHR** in **Christ** and **Christmas** and **SCH** in school are trigraphs (or digraph blends). They are a combination of the digraph **CH** and the letters **R** or **S**. See the **CHR** and **SCH** lists in the Trigraphs section for more **CH** words.

See next page for word lists.

ch

choir

Base	LT's	-s/-es	-ed	-ing	-y/-ly	-er	-est
ache	a-e	aches	ached	aching	achy	*achier*	*achiest*
*chasm***		chasms					
choir	oi*	choirs					
chord	or	chords					
loch**		lochs					
*schism***		schisms					
tech		techs					

Even though the words **chasm and **schism** sound like they have two syllables, there is only one vowel sound in each word, and therefore they are single-syllable words.

In the United States, the word **loch is usually pronounced with the /k/ sound. However, in some areas, especially in Scottish English, the **CH** has more of a backward throat sound.

Compound

Base	LT's	-s/-es	-ed	-ing	-y/-ly	-er	-est
backache	ck a-e	backaches					
bellyache	ll -y a-e	bellyaches					
earache	ear a-e	earaches					
headache	ea a-e	headaches					
heartache	ear* a-e	heartaches					
stomachache	o* a-e	stomachaches					
toothache	oo th a-e	toothaches					

ch

/sh/ in chute

Position: Beginning and End

Vocalization: Unvoiced

Classification: Digraph

Group: H-Brothers

Multiple spellings (common) /sh/: SH

Multiple spellings (rare) /sh/: <u>CH</u>

Multiple sounds for CH: /ch/ in chess, /k/ in choir, <u>/sh/ in chute</u>

- **CH** has three different sounds. **CH** says **/ch/** in **chair** in most English words. It also says **/k/** in words of Greek origin, like **chord**, and **/sh/** in words of French origin, like **charade**.
- The words in this list say **/sh/** and are mostly of French origin. They are complex words, and therefore they are better suited for more advanced learners.
- When **CH** says **/sh/** is at the end of a word, it is usually combined with **E** to make **CHE (creche, quiche)**.

See next page for word lists.

ch

chute

Base	LT's	-s/-es	-ed	-ing	-y/-ly	-er	-est
cache	e*	caches					
chic	i*					chicer	chicest
chute	u-e	chutes					
creche	cr e-e*	creches					
fiche	i-e*						
gauche	au* e*						
quiche	qu* i-e*						

Multi-syllable

Base	LT's	-s/-es	-ed	-ing
brochure	br ure	brochures		
cachet*	sh e* t*	cashets		
chalet*	e* t*	chalets		
chaperone	er o-e	chaperones	chaperoned	chaperoning
chateaux*	eau x*			
Chicago				
crochet*	cr e* t*	crochets		
fuchsia*	s* i*			
machete*	e-e*	machetes		
machine*	i-e*	machines	machined	machining
panache*	a-e*			
touche*	ou* e*			

*Many of these words are from French origins, so the letters may be pronounced differently.

/g/ in ghost

Position: Beginning and End

Vocalization: Voiced

Classification: Digraph

Group: H-Brothers or Silent H

Multiple spellings (common) /g/: G, GU

Multiple spellings (rare) /g/: -GUE, GH

Multiple sounds for GH: /g/ in ghost*

*GH as a part of other longer letter teams also says **/f/** in **laugh (AUGH)** and is **/silent/** in **sigh/sight**
(IGH/IGHT) and dough **(OUGH)**

- In the **GH** words in this list, the **G** is expressed, and the **H** remains silent.
- **GH** is a part of several complicated letter teams. In some letter teams, **GH** is silent **(IGH-sigh, IGHT-night, EIGHT-eight, OUGH-dough).** In other letter teams, **GH** says **/f/ (OUGH-cough).**
- In compound words, two letters next to each other may appear to be a digraph but are in fact letters from two separate words. lon**g** + **h**orn = longhorn (not digraph **GH**), an**t** + **h**ill = anthill (not digraph **TH**).

Base	LT's	-s/-es	-ed	-ing
burgh	ur	burghs		
ghee	ee			
ghost	st	ghosts	ghosted	ghosting
ghoul	ou	ghouls		
ugh				

gh

ghost

Multi-syllable

Base	LT's	-s/-es	-ed	-ing	-y/-ly	-er	-est
ghastly	st -ly					ghastlier	ghastliest
gherkin	er	gherkins					
ghetto		ghettos					
ghoulish	ou sh				ghoulishly		
Pittsburgh	ur						

ph

/f/ in phone

Position: Beginning and End

Vocalization: Unvoiced

Classification: Digraph

Group: H-Brothers

Multiple spellings (common) /f/:   F, PH, FF

Multiple spellings (rare) /f/:   GH

Multiple sounds for PH: Only /f/ in phone

- Words with **PH** have Greek origins. **PH** represents the Greek letter **phi**- Φ.
- **PH** words are uncommon, so if students are unsure about spelling, they should always try the spelling **F** for **/f/** before trying **PH**.
- In compound words, two letters next to each other may appear to be a digraph but are in fact letters from two separate words. to**p** + **h**at = tophat (not digraph **PH**), an**t** + **h**ill = anthill (not digraph **TH**).

Base	LT's	-s/-es	-ed	-ing	-y/-ly	-er	-est
graph	gr	graphs	graphed	graphing			
humph							
lymph	y						
morph	or	morphs	morphed	morphing			
nymph	y	nymphs					
oomph	oo						
phase	a-e	phases	phased	phasing			
phew	ew						
phone	o-e	phones	phoned	phoning			
phrase	a-e	phrases	phrased	phrasing			

ph

Compound

Base	LT's	-s/-es	-ed
catchphrase	tch a-e	catchphrases	
cellphone	ll o-e	cellphones	
earphone	ear o-e	earphones	
phonecard	o-e ar	phonecards	
videophone	o-e	videophones	
sousaphone	ou o-e	sousaphones	
payphone	ay o-e	payphones	
speakerphone	sp ea er o-e	speakerphones	

Multi-syllable

Base	LT's	-s/-es	-ed	-ing
telephone	o-e	telephones	telephoned	telephoning
gramophone	gr o-e	gramophones		
homophone	o-e	homophones		
Philadelphia	i*			
Phillies	ll i* -es			
saxophone	o-e	saxophones		
xylophone	x y* o-e	xylophones		

<u>rh</u>

/r/ in rhino

Position: Beginning and End

Vocalization: Voiced

Classification: Digraph

Group: H Brothers or Silent H

Multiple spellings (common) /r/: R

Multiple spellings (rare) /r/: WR, <u>RH</u>

Multiple sounds for RH: <u>Only /r/ in rhino</u>

- **RH** was originally used in Latin to spell the Greek letter Rho, which looks like a capital **P**, but says the **/r/** sound.
- **RH** is not common in single syllable words, but it is used in several multi-syllable words.
- In compound words, two letters next to each other may appear to be a digraph but are in fact letters from two separate words. ove**r** + **h**eat = overheat (not digraph **RH**), an**t** + **h**ill = anthill (not digraph **TH**).

Base	LT's	-s/-es	-ed	-ing	-y/-ly	-er	-est
myrrh	y						
rhyme	y-e	rhymes	rhymed	rhyming			

Multi-syllable

Base	LT's	-s/-es	-ed	-ing	-y/-ly	-er	-est
biorhythm	y th	biorhythms					
catarrh	ar						
cirrhosis	ir						
diarrhea	ar						
hemorrhage	or g(e)	hemorrhages					

Multi-syllable

Base	LT's	-s/-es	-ed	-ing	-y/-ly	-er	-est
hemorrhoid	or oi	hemorrhoids					
rhapsodic	-ic						
rhapsody	y	rhapsodies					
rhesus							
rhetoric	or -ic				rhetorically		
rhetorical	or -ic						
rheumatic	eu -ic						
rheumatism	eu sm						
rhinestone	i-e st o-e	rhinestones					
rhino		rhinos					
rhinoceros	c (e)	rhinoceroses*					
rhizome	o-e	rhizomes					
rhododendron	dr	rhododendrons					
rhombus		rhombuses					
rhubarb	ar	rhubarbs					
rhythm	y th	rhythms					
rhythmic	y th -ic				rhythmically		

*Rhinoceros can become a plural by either remaining rhinoceros or adding -es.

sh

/sh/ in ship

Position: Beginning and End

Vocalization: Unvoiced

Classification: Digraph

Group: H-Brothers

Multiple spellings (common) /sh/: SH,

Multiple spellings (rare) /sh/: CH

Multiple sounds for SH: Only /sh/ in ship

- **SH** sometimes combines with **R** to make the trigraph (or digraph blend), **SHR**. See the **SHR** list in the trigraphs section for more **SH** words.
- Words that end in **/sh/** create a plural by adding **-ES**, instead of **-S (wash – washes)**.
- In compound or multi-syllable words, two letters next to each other may appear to be a digraph but are in fact letters from two separate words. mi**s**+**h**eard = misheard (not digraph **SH**), an**t** + **h**ill = anthill (not digraph **TH**).

Base	LT's	-s/-es	-ed	-ing	-y/-ly	-er	-est
ash		ashes			ashy		
bash		bashes	bashed	bashing			
blush	bl	blushes	blushed	blushing		blusher	
brash	br				brashly	brasher	brashest
brush	br	brushes	brushed	brushing			
bush	u	bushes	bushed	bushing	bushy	bushier	bushiest
cash		cashes	cashed	cashing			
clash	cl	clashes	clashed	clashing			
crash	cr	crashes	crashed	crashing			
crush	cr	crushes	crushed	crushing		crusher	
dash		dashes	dashed	dashing		Dasher	
dish		dishes	dished	dishing			

sh

Base	LT's	-s/-es	-ed	-ing	-y/-ly	-er	-est
fish		fishes	fished	fishing	fishy	fisher	
flash	fl	flashes	flashed	flashing	flashy	flasher	
flush	fl	flushes	flushed	flushing		flusher	
fresh	fr				freshly	fresher	freshest
gash		gashes	gashed	gashing			
gnash	gn	gnashes	gnashed	gnashing			
gush		gushes	gushed	gushing	gushy	gusher	
harsh	ar				harshly	harsher	harshest
hash		hashes	hashed	hashing			
hush		hushes	hushed	hushing			
Josh		Josh's					
lash		lashes	lashed	lashing		lasher	
leash	ea	leashes	leashed	leashing			
lush						lusher	lushest
marsh	ar	marshes			marshy	marshier	marshiest
mash		mashes	mashed	mashing		masher	
mesh		meshes	meshed	meshing			
mush		mushes	mushed	mushing	mushy	mushier	mushiest
plush	pl						
posh							
push	u	pushes	pushed	pushing	pushy	pushier	pushiest
rash		rashes					
sash		sashes					
shack	ck	shacks	shacked	shacking			
shade	a-e	shades	shaded	shading	shady	shadier	shadiest
shaft	ft	shafts	shafted	shafting			
shake	a-e	shakes		shaking	shaky	shakier	shakiest
shale	a-e						
sham		shams					
shame	a-e						
shape	a-e	shapes	shaped	shaping			
shard	ar	shards					
share	are	shares	shared	sharing		sharer	
shark	ar	sharks			sharky		
sharp	ar	sharps			sharply	sharper	sharpest
shave	a-e	shaves	shaved	shaving		shaver	
shawl	aw	shawls					
she	sh e						
sheaf	ea	sheaves					
shear	ear	shears	sheared	shearing		shearer	

Base	LT's	-s/-es	-ed	-ing	-y/-ly	-er	-est
sheath	ea th	sheaths	sheathed	sheathing			
shed		sheds		shedding		shedder	
sheen	ee						
sheep	ee						
sheer	eer	sheers	sheered	sheering		sheerer	sheerest
sheet	ee	sheets	sheeted	sheeting			
shelf	lf	shelves	shelved	shelving			
shell	ll	shells	shelled	shelling	Shelly	sheller	
shin		shins					
shine	i-e	shines	shined	shining	shiny	shiner/*shinier*	*shiniest*
ship		ships	shipped	shipping		shipper	
shire	ire	shires					
shirk	ir	shirks	shirked	shirking		shirker	
shirt	ir	shirts					
shoal	oa	shoals					
shock	ck	shocks	shocked	shocking		shocker	
shod							
shoe	oe*	shoes	shoed	shoeing			
shone	o-e						
shoo	oo	shoos	shooed	shooing			
shook	oo						
shoot	oo	shoots		shooting		shooter	
shop		shops	shopped	shopping		shopper	
shore	ore	shores	shored	shoring			
shorn	or						
short	or	shorts	shorted	shorting	shorty	shorter	shortest
shot		shots					
shout	ou	shouts	shouted	shouting		shouter	
shove	o* ve	shoves	shoved	shoving			
show	ow	shows	showed	showing	showy	*showier*	*showiest*
shown	ow						
shuck	ck	shucks	shucked	shucking		shucker	
shun		shuns	shunned	shunning			
shunt	nt	shunts	shunted	shunting			
shush		shushes	shushed	shushing			
shut		shuts		shutting		shutter	
shy	y	shies	shied	shying	shyly	shyer	shyest
slash	sl	slashes	slashed	slashing		slasher	
slosh	sl	sloshes	sloshed	sloshing	sloshy	*sloshier*	*sloshiest*
slush	sl	slushes	slushed	slushing	slushy	*slushier*	*slushiest*

sh

Base	LT's	-s/-es	-ed	-ing	-y/-ly	-er	-est
smash	sm	smashes	smashed	smashing		smasher	
splash	spl	splashes	splashed	splashing	splashy	*splashier*	*splashiest*
squash	squ/qua	squashes	squashed	squashing			
squish	squ	squishes	squished	squishing	squishy	*squishier*	*squishiest*
stash	st	stashes	stashed	stashing		stasher	
swish	sw	swishes	swished	swishing	swishy	*swishier*	*swishiest*
thrash	thr	thrashes	thrashed	thrashing			
thresh	thr	threshes	threshed	threshing		thresher	
thrush	thr	thrushes					
trash	tr	trashes	trashed	trashing	trashy	*trashier*	*trashiest*
tush	u				tushy		
wash	wa	washes	washed	washing		washer	
wish		wishes	wished	wishing		wisher	

Compound

Base	LT's	s/s/-es	-ed	-ing
airship	air	airships		
ashtray	tr ay	ashtrays		
backlash	ck	backlashes		
battleship	tle	battleships		
bloodshed	oo bl			
bookshop	oo	bookshops		
brainwash	br wa ai	brainwashes	brainwashed	brainwashing
brushwood	br oo			
brushwork	br wor			
courtship	our	courtships		
crayfish	cr ay	crayfishes		
dashboard	oar	dashboards		
dishcloth	cl th	dishcloths		
dishpan		dishpans		
dishrag		dishrags		
dishwater	wa -er			
dogfish		dogfishes		
downshift	ow ft	downshifts		
earshot	ear			
eggshell	gg* ll	eggshells		

Compound, continued

Base	LT's	-s/-es	-ed	-ing	-y/-ly
eyelash	e-e*	eyelashes			
fishbowl	ow	fishbowls			
fishnet		fishnets			
flashback	fl ck	flashbacks			
flashbulb	fl	flashbulbs			
flashcard	fl ar	flashcards			
flashlight	fl ight	flashlights			
flashpoint	fl oi nt	flashpoints			
freshman	fr				
gearshift	ear ft	gearshifts			
goldfish	old				
gumshoe	oe*	gumshoes			
gunshot		gunshots			
handshake	nd a-e	handshakes			
hardship	ar	hardships			
horseshoe	or -se oe*	horseshoes			
hotshot		hotshots			
kinship					
ladyship	y	ladyships			
lampshade	mp a-e	lampshades			
lordship	or	lordships			
makeshift	a-e ft				
milkshake	lk a-e	milkshakes			
moonshine	oo i-e				
mouthwash	ou th wa	mouthwashes			
newsflash	ew fl -s	newsflashes			
nightshirt	ight ir	nightshirts			
outshine	ou i-e	outshines			
overshadow	er ow	overshadows			
overshoot	er oo	overshoots			
paintbrush	ai nt br	paintbrushes			
pawnshop	aw	pawnshops			
plowshare	pl ow are	plowshares			
pushcart	ar u	pushcarts			
rickshaw	ck aw	rickshaws			
roadshow	oa ow	roadshows			
seashell	ea ll	seashells			
shakedown	a-e ow	shakedowns			
shakeout	a-e ou				
shameless	a-e ss				shamelessly

Compound

Base	LT's	-s/-es	-ed	-ing	-y/-ly	-er
shamrock	ck	shamrocks				
shapeless	a-e ss				shapelessly	
sheepdog	ee	sheepdogs				
shellfish	ll	shellfishes				
shinbone	o-e	shinbones				
shipmate	a-e	shipmates				
shipshape	a-e					
shipwreck	wr ck	shipwrecks	shipwrecked	shipwrecking		
shockproof	ck pr oo					
shoehorn	oe* or	shoehorns				
shoelace	oe* a-e ce	shoelaces				
shopfront	fr nt o	shopfronts				
shoplift	ft	shoplifts	shoplifted	shoplifting		shoplifter
shortbread	or br ea	shortbreads				
shortcake	or a-e	shortcakes				
shorthand	or nd		shorthanded			
shortlist	or st		shortlisted	shortlisting		
showboat	ow oa	showboats				
showplace	ow pl ace	showplaces				
showroom	ow oo	showrooms				
shutdown	ow	shutdowns				
shutout	ou	shutouts				
slapdash	sl					
slingshot	sl ing	slingshots				
slipshod	sl					
snowshoe	sn ow oe*	snowshoes				
spaceship	sp ace	spaceships				
starfish	st ar	starfishes				
steamship	st ea	steamships				
sunshine	i-e				sunshiny	
sweatshirt	ea sw ir	sweatshirts				
sweatshop	sw ea	sweatshops				
timeshare	i-e are	timeshares				
toothbrush	oo th br	toothbrushes				
township	ow	townships				
trashcan	tr	trashcans				
upshot		upshots				
washbowl	wa ow	washbowls				
washcloth	wa cl th	washcloths				

Compound, continued

Base	LT's	-s/-es	-ed	-ing
washout	wa ou	washouts		
washroom	wa oo	washrooms		
washstand	wa st nd	washstands		
whiplash	wh	whiplashes	whiplashed	whiplashing
whitewash	wh i-e wa	whitewashes	whitewashed	whitewashing
wishbone	o-e	wishbones		
woodshed	oo	woodsheds		
worksheet	wor ee	worksheets		
workshop	wor	workshops		

th

/th/ in thing

Position: Beginning and End

Vocalization: Unvoiced

Classification: Digraph

Group: H-brothers

Multiple spellings /th/: Only TH

Multiple sounds for TH: unvoiced /th/ in thing, voiced /th/ in that

- **TH** has two sounds, **/th/** in **thing** and **/th/** in **that**. The **TH** in **thing** is **unvoiced** because the sound is only formed in the mouth, and not the throat. The **TH** in **that** is **voiced** because the sound is partially formed in the throat/larynx as the vocal cords vibrate. In both cases, the tongue touches the back of the teeth.
- This list is for the unvoiced **/th/** in **thing** sound. Unvoiced **/th/** in **thing** is more common than voiced **/th/** in **that**.
- **TH** is combined with **R** to make the trigraph (or digraph blend) **THR**. See the **THR** list in the Trigraphs section for more **TH** words.
- When **E** is added to the end of a word that ends in unvoiced **TH** in **thin**, the sound changes to voiced **TH** in **THIS** (**bath – bathe, teeth – teethe**). This change also transforms a noun to a verb.
- When the endings -**ERN, -Y,** and -**ERLY** are added to the end of an unvoiced **TH** word, the **TH** changes to voiced. (**north – northern, worth – worthy** (Venezky, 1999)
- When a word that ends in **TH** becomes plural by adding -**ES**, it often changes from an unvoiced **TH** to a voiced **TH**. (**seeth – seethes, cloth – clothes**).
- In compound words, two letters next to each other may appear to be a digraph but are in fact letters from two separate words. foo**t** + **h**ills = foothills (not digraph **PH**), an**t** + **h**ill = anthill (not digraph **TH**).

th

thing

Base	LT's	-s/-es/'s	-ed	-ing	-y/-ly	-er	-est
bath		baths/bathes	bathed	bathing		bather	
berth	er	berths					
Beth		Beth's					
birth	ir	births	birthed	birthing			
Blythe	y-e bl	Blythe's					
booth	oo	booths					
both	o*						
broth	br	broths					
cloth	cl	clothes	clothed	clothing			
dearth	ear						
death	ea	deaths					
depth		depths					
doth							
earth	ear	earths			earthly		
eighth	eigh	eighths					
faith	ai	faiths					
Faith		Faith's					
forth	or						
fourth	our						
froth	fr	froths	frothed	frothing			
Garth	ar	Garth's					
girth	ir						
growth	gr ow	growths					
hath							
health	ea				healthy	*healthier*	*healthiest*
Heath	ea	Heath's					
Keith	ei	Keith's					
length	ng	lengths			lengthy	*lengthier*	*lengthiest*
math							
mirth	ir						
month	o	months			monthly		
moth		moths					
mouth	ou	mouths	mouthed	mouthing	mouthy	*mouthier*	*mouthiest*
myth	y	myths					
ninth							
north**	or						
North**	or	North's					

*The word **north** is capitalized only when it refers to the proper name of a region, such as the **North Pole**, or **North Dakota**. When the word **north** refers to a general direction, such as in the sentence, "The United States and Canada are located **north** of the equator," the word **north** is not capitalized.

th

thing

Base	LT's	-s/-es	-ed	-ing	-y/-ly	-er	-est
oath	oa	oaths					
path		paths					
Ruth	u	Ruth's					
Seth		Seth's					
sheath	sh ea	sheaths					
sloth	sl	sloths					
Smith	sm	Smith's					
south**	ou						
South**	ou	South's					
swath	sw a*	swaths					
teeth	ee	teethes	teethed	teething		teether	
tenth		tenths					
thank	ank	thanks	thanked	thanking			
thatch	tch	thatches	thatched	thatching			
thaw	aw	thaws	thawed	thawing			
theft	ft	thefts					
theme	e-e	themes					
thick	ck				thickly	thicker	thickest
thief	ie	thieves	thieved	thieving			
thigh	igh	thighs					
thin					thinly	thinner	thinnest
thing	ing	things					
think	ink	thinks		thinking		thinker	
third	ir						
thirst	ir st	thirsts	thirsted	thirsting	thirsty	*thirstier*	*thirstiest*
thorn	or	thorns	thorned		thorny	*thornier*	*thorniest*
Thor		Thor's					
thug		thugs					
thumb	mb	thumbs	thumbed	thumbing			
thump	mp	thumps	thumped	thumping			
tooth	oo				toothy	*toothier*	*toothiest*
truth	tr u	truths					
warmth	war th						

The word **south is capitalized only when it refers to the proper name of a region, such as the **South Pole**, or **South Dakota**. When the word **south** refers to a general direction, such as, "Australia is located **south** of the equator," the word **south** is not capitalized.

thing

Base	LT's	-s/-es	-ed	-ing	-y/-ly	-er	-est
wealth	ea th				wealthy	*wealthier*	*wealthiest*
width							
worth	wor				worthy	*worthier*	*worthiest*
wrath	wr						
wreath	wr ea	wreaths					
youth	ou	youths					

Compound

Base	LT's	-s/-es	-ed	-ing	-y/-ly	-er	-est
bathrobe	o-e	bathrobes					
bathroom	oo	bathrooms					

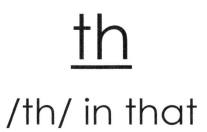

/th/ in that

Position: Beginning and End

Vocalization: Voiced

Classification: Digraph

Group: H-brothers

Multiple spellings /r/: <u>Only TH</u>

Multiple sounds for TH: unvoiced /th/ in thing, <u>voiced /th/ in that</u>

- **TH** has two sounds, **/th/** in **thing** and **/th/** in **that**. The **TH** in **thing** is **unvoiced** because the sound is only formed in the mouth, and not the throat. The **TH** in **that** is **voiced** because the sound is partially formed in the throat as the vocal cords vibrate. In both cases, the tongue touches the back of the teeth.
- This list is for the voiced **/th/** in **that** sound. Unvoiced **/th/** in **thing** is much more common than voiced **/th/** in **that**.
- For **VCE** words, the **O-E, (clothe), I-E (tithe)**, etc. spans the two letters of **TH**, because **TH** counts as one sound.
- When **E** is added to the end of a word that ends in unvoiced **TH** in **thin**, the sound changes to voiced **TH** in **THIS** (**bath – bathe, teeth – teethe**). This change also transforms a noun to a verb.
- When the endings- **ERN, -Y,** and **-ERLY** are added to the end of an unvoiced **TH**, the **TH** changes to voiced. (**north – northern, worth – worthy** (Venezky, 1999)
- When a word ending in **TH** becomes plural by adding - **ES**, it often changes from an unvoiced **TH** to a voiced **TH**. (**booth – booths, cloth – clothes**).
- In compound words, two letters next to each other may appear to be a digraph but are in fact letters from two separate words. foo**t** + **h**ills = foothills (not digraph **TH**), an**t** + **h**ill = anthill (not digraph **TH**).

Beginning

Base	LT's	-s/-es	-ed	-ing	-y/-ly	-er	-est
than							
that							
the**							
thee	ee						
their	eir	theirs					
them							
then							
*there**	ere*						
these	e-e						
they	ey						
thine	i-e						
this							
those	o-e						
thou	ou						
though	ough						
thus					thusly		
thy	y						
tithe	i-e	tithes	tithed	tithing		tither	
with							

****The** can be pronounced /**thee**/ or /**thuh**/.

End

Base	LT's	-s/-es	-ed	-ing	-y/-ly	-er	-est
bathe	a-e e*	bathes	bathed	bathing		bather	
clothe	cl o-e	clothes	clothed	clothing			
seethe	ee e*	seethes	seethed	seething			
smooth	sm oo	smooths	smoothed	smoothing	smoothly	smoother	smoothest
teethe	ee e*	teethes	teethed	teething		teether	

Compound

Base	LT's	-s/-es	-ed	-ing	-y/-ly	-er	-est
clothespin	cl -es	clothespins					
otherwise	er i-e						
seaworthy	ea wor -y						
withdraw	dr aw	withdraws		withdrawing			
withdrawn	dr aw						
withstand	st nd	withstands		withstanding			

whale

/w/ or /hw/ in whale

Position: Beginning

Vocalization: Voiced

Classification: Digraph

Group: H-brothers or Silent H (in some dialects)

Multiple spellings (common) /W/: W, <u>WH</u>

Multiple sounds for WH: <u>/w/ or /hw/ in whale</u>, /h/ in who

- **WH** was originally pronounced with a slight breath that we label **/hw/**, instead of **/w/**. This difference has become almost indistinguishable in most regions with English speakers, and children often pronounce words that have **WH** in them just as **/w/**. In some areas, the **/hw/** is still spoken. If you live in one of these areas, you can tell the children to hold their hand in front of their lips, and they may be able to feel the puff of air that distinguishes **WH** from **W.**
- **WH** is also pronounced **/h/** in a few words **(who)**, which have their own list on the next page. However, the majority of **WH** words say **/w/**.
- **WH** is used frequently in question words **(what, when**...).
- **WH** is used frequently in words related to noises or sounds **(wham, whack, whine...),** and in words that are related to movement **(whir, whizz, whisk...)** (Bishop, 1986)
- **WH** is never used at the end of a word.
- In compound words, two letters next to each other may appear to be a digraph but are in fact letters from two separate words. blo**w**+**h**ole = blowhole (not digraph **WH**), an**t** + **h**ill = anthill (not digraph **TH**).

41

wh

whale

Base	LT's	-s/-es	-ed	-ing	-y/-ly	-er	-est
whack	ck	whacks	whacked	whacking			
whale	a-e	whales				whaler	
wham		whams	whammed	whamming			
wharf	ar	wharfs					
*what**	a*						
wheat	ea						
wheel	ee	wheels	wheeled	wheeling			
wheeze	ee -ze	wheezes	wheezed	wheezing	wheezy		
when							
*where**	ere*						
whet		whets	whetted	whetting			
whey	ey						
which	ch						
whiff	ff	whiffs	whiffed	whiffing			
whim		whims					
whine	i-e	whines	whined	whining	whiny	whiner/*whinier*	*whiniest*
whip		whips	whipped	whipping			
whir	ir	whirrs	whirred	whirring			
whirl	ir	whirls	whirled	whirling	whirly		
whisk	sk	whisks	whisked	whisking			
white	i-e					whiter	whitest
whiz							
whizz	zz	whizzes	whizzed	whizzing			
whoa	oa						
whoop	oo	whoops	whooped	whooping			
whoosh	oo sh	whooshes	whooshed	whooshing			
whop		whops	whopped	whopping		whopper	
why	y						

See next page for compound words.

42

wh

whale

Compound

Base	LT's	-s/-es	-ed	-ing	-y/-ly	-er	-est
*anywhere**	-y ere*						
buckwheat	ck ea						
bullwhip	ull	bullwhips					
cartwheel	ar ee	cartwheels					
flywheel	fl y ee	flywheels					
meanwhile	ea i-e						
nowhere	ere*						
pinwheel	ee	pinwheels					
somewhat	o-e*						
somewhere	o-e* ere						
wheatgerm	ea er g(e)						
wheelchair	ee ch ai	wheelchairs					
wheelhouse	ee ou -se	wheelhouses					
whenever	er						
wherever	er ere						
whirlpool	ir oo	whirlpools					
whirlwind	ir nd	whirlwinds					
whiteboard	i-e oar	whiteboards					
whitecap	i-e	whitecaps					
whiteout	i-e ou	whiteouts					
whitewash	i-e wa sh	whitewashes	whitewashed	whitewashing			

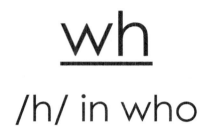

/h/ in who

Position: Beginning

Vocalization: Unvoiced

Classification: Digraph

Group: H-brothers or Silent H

Multiple spellings (common) /h/: H

Multiple spellings (rare) /h/: <u>WH</u>

Multiple sounds for WH: /w/ or /hw/ in whale, <u>/h/ in who</u>

- The **/w/** sound in **whale** is used in most words. The **/h/** sound in in **who** is rare.
- In compound words, two letters next to each other may appear to be a digraph but are in fact letters from two separate words. blo**w**+**h**ole = blowhole (not digraph **WH**), an**t** + **h**ill = anthill (not digraph **TH**).

Base	LT's	-s/-es/'s	-ed	-ing	-y/-ly	-er	-est
*who**	o*	who's					
whole	o-e						
*whom**	o*						

Compound

Base	LT's		-s/-es	-ed	-ing	-y/-ly	-er	-est
whoever	er							
wholegrain	o-e	gr ai	wholegrains					
wholesale	o-e	a-e						
wholesome*	o-e	o-e*						
whomever	er							

Trigraphs & 3 letter blends
Printable Cards

chr	sch
scr	shr

spl	spr
squ	str

thr

chr

/kr/ in Christmas

Position: Beginning

Vocalization: Voiced

Classification: Trigraph or Digraph Blend

Group: Trigraph or Digraph Blend

Multiple spellings (common): CR

Multiple spellings (rare): CHR

Multiple sounds for CHR: Only /kr/

- **CHR** is uncommon in one-syllable words, so some educators do not teach it as a separate trigraph. However, **CHR** is also used in multi-syllable words, so learning it can be useful.
- Some programs will refer to this type of Trigraph as a Digraph Blend, since it is blending a digraph with another consonant.
- **CHR** words come from primarily three sources. The first is faith-based words, that are derived from the word **Christ (christen, Christian, Christmas)**. The second source is from the Greek root **chrom**, which means color **(monochrome)**. The third source is the Greek root **chronos**, which means time **(chronology)**.

CHR words

Base	LT's	-s/-es/'s	-ed	-ing	-y/-ly	-er	-est
Chris		Chris'					
Christ	st	Christ's					

See next page for multi-syllable.

Multi-syllable

Base	LT's	-s/-es/'s	-ed	-ing
*christen**	st*	christens	christened	christening
Christian	st	Christians/Christian's		
Christmas	st*	Christmases		
Christopher	st ph er	Christopher's		
chromatic	-ic			
*chromium**	i*			
chromosome	o-e	chromosomes		
chronic	-ic			
chronicle	cle -ic	chronicles	chronicled	chronicling
chronology	g(y) -y	chronologies		
chrysalis	y	chrysalises		

sch

/sk/ in school

Position: Beginning

Vocalization: Unvoiced

Classification: Trigraph or Digraph Blend

Group: Trigraph or Digraph Blend

Multiple spellings(common)/sk/: SC, SK

Multiple spellings (rare) /sk/: SCH

Multiple sounds for SCH: Only /sk/

- **SCH** is a trigraph. It is a combination of the digraph **CH** that says **/k/**, and the letter **S**. Some programs may call it a Digraph Blend.
- The **SCH** spelling is rare, so students who are unsure about a spelling should try **SK** or **SC** first when they are attempting to spell a **/sk/** word.
- **SCH** words may have derived from several sources, including Middle English **(sch)**, Latin **(sch)** and Greek **(skh)**, (etymonline.com)

Base	LT's	-s/-es	-ed	-ing	-y/-ly	-er	-est
scheme	e-e	schemes	schemed	scheming		schemer	
schism	sm	schisms					
school	oo	schools	schooled	schooling			

See next page for compound words.

Compound

Base	LT's	-s/-es	-ed	-ing	-y/-ly	-er	-est
playschool	pl ay oo						
schoolbag	oo	schoolbags					
schoolchild	oo ch ild						
schoolhouse	oo ou -se	schoolhouses					
schoolkid	oo	schoolkids					
schoolmate	oo a-e	schoolmates					
schoolwork	oo wor						
schoolyard	oo ar	schoolyards					

scr

/skr/ in scrape

Position: Beginning

Vocalization: Voiced

Classification: Three letter blend

Group: Trigraph

Multiple spellings (rare) /skr/: <u>Only SCR</u>

Multiple sounds for SCR: <u>Only /skr/</u>

- **SCR** is a three-letter blend. The **S, C** and **R** retain their original sounds.
- Many **SCR** words refer to struggle or violence **(scrape, scratch, scream).** They also refer to writing **(scrawl, scribe, script).**

Base	LT's	-s/-es	-ed	-ing	-y/-ly	-er	-est
scram		scrams	scrammed	scramming			
scrap		scraps	scrapped	scrapping		scrapper	
scrape	a-e	scrapes	scraped	scraping		scraper	
scratch	tch	scratches	scratched	scratching		scratcher	
scrawl	aw	scrawls	scrawled	scrawling			
scream	ea	screams	screamed	screaming		screamer	
screech	ee ch	screeches	screeched	screeching			
screen	ee	screens	screened	screening		screener	
screw	ew	screws	screwed	screwing			
scribe	i-e	scribes	scribed	scribing			
scrimp	mp	scrimps	scrimped	scrimping			
script	pt	scripts	scripted	scripting			
scroll	oll	scrolls	scrolled	scrolling			
scrub		scrubs	scrubbed	scrubbing	scrubby	scrubber	
scruff	ff				scruffy	*scruffier*	*scruffiest*

See next page for SCR Compound Words.

scr

Compound

Base	LT's	-s/-es	-ed	-ing	-y/-ly	-er	-est
corkscrew	or ew	corkscrews					
postscript	ost pt	postscripts					
scrapbook	oo	scrapbooks					
scrapheap	ea	scrapheaps					
scratchpad	tch	scratchpads					
screenplay	ee pl ay	screenplays					
skyscraper	y a-e sk er	skyscrapers					
smokescreen	o-e ee sm	smokescreens					
transcript	tr pt	transcripts					
typescript	y-e pt	typescripts					
widescreen	i-e ee	widescreens					

shr

/shr/ in shred

Position: Beginning

Vocalization: Voiced

Classification: Trigraph or Digraph Blend

Group: Trigraph or Digraph Blend

Multiple spellings (rare)/shr/: <u>Only SHR</u>

Multiple sounds for SHR: <u>Only /shr/</u>

- **SHR** is a trigraph. It's a combination of the digraph **SH**, and the letter **R**. Some programs will refer to this kind of combination as a Digraph Blend.

Base	LT's	-s/-es	-ed	-ing	-y/-ly	-er	-est
shrank	ank						
shred		shreds	shredded	shredding		shredder	
shrew	ew	shrews					
shrewd	ew				shrewdly		
shriek	ie	shrieks	shrieked	shrieking			
shrill	ll				shrilly	shriller	shrillest
shrimp	mp	shrimps	shrimped	shrimping			
shrine	i-e	shrines	shrined	shrining			
shrink	ink	shrinks		shrinking			
shroud	ou	shrouds	shrouded	shrouding			
shrub		shrubs					
shrug		shrugs	shrugged	shrugging			
shrunk	unk						

spl

/spl/ in split

Position: Beginning

Vocalization: Voiced

Classification: Three-letter Blend

Group: Trigraph

Multiple spellings (rare) /spl/: Only SPL

Multiple sounds for SPL: Only /spl/

- **SPL** is a three-letter blend. The **S, P**, and **L** all retain their original sounds.
- Most **SPL** words are dramatic actions **(splash, splay, splurge)**

Base	LT's	-s/-es	-ed	-ing	-y/-ly	-er	-est
splash	sh	splashes	splashed	splashing	splashy		
splat		splats	splatted	splatting		splatter	
splay	ay	splays	splayed	splaying			
spleen	ee	spleens					
splice	ice	splices	spliced	splicing			
splint	nt	splints	splinted	splinting		splinter	
split		splits		splitting		splitter	
splotch	tch	splotches	splotched	splotching	splotchy	splotchier	splotchiest
splurge	ur ge	splurges	splurged	splurging			

Compound

Base	LT's	-s/-es	-ed	-ing	-y/-ly	-er	-est
logsplitter	er	logsplitters					

spr

/spr/ in spray

Position: Beginning

Vocalization: Voiced

Classification: Three-letter Blend

Group: Trigraph

Multiple spellings (rare) /spr/: Only SPR

Multiple sounds for SPR: Only /spr/

- **SPR** is a three-letter blend. The **S, P,** and **R** all retain their original sounds.
- Most **SPR** words refer to dramatic actions **(sprang, sprawl, spread)**

Base	LT's	-s/-es	-ed	-ing	-y/-ly	-er	-est
sprain	ai	sprains	sprained	spraining			
sprang	ang						
sprawl	aw	sprawls	sprawled	sprawling			
spray	ay	sprays	sprayed	spraying		sprayer	
spread	ea	spreads		spreading		spreader	
spree	ee	sprees					
sprig		sprigs					
spring	ing	springs		springing	springy	springier	springiest
sprint	nt	sprints	sprinted	sprinting		sprinter	
sprite	i-e	sprites			spritely		
spritz	tz	spritzes	spritzed	spritzing		spritzer	
sprout	ou	sprouts	sprouted	sprouting			
spruce	uce	spruces	spruced	sprucing			
sprung	ng						
spry	y				spryly		

See next page for Compound words.

Compound

Base	LT's	-s/-es	-ed	-ing	-y/-ly	-er	-est
beansprout	ea ou	beansprouts					
bedspread	ea	bedspreads					
hairspray	air ay	hairsprays					
offspring	ff ing						
spreadsheet	sh ea ee	spreadsheets					
springboard	ing oar	springboards					
springtime	ing i-e						
wellspring	ll ing						
widespread	i-e ea						

SQU

/skw/ in square

Position: Beginning

Vocalization: Voiced

Classification: Trigraph or Digraph Blend

Group: Trigraph

Multiple spellings (rare) /skw/: Only SQU

Multiple sounds for SQU: Only /skw/

- **SQU** is either a trigraph or a three-letter blend, depending on whether **QU** is considered a digraph or a blend. The **S** is combined with **QU.**
- Most **SQU** words are either loud sounds **(squawk, squeal)** or action verbs **(squash, squirm)**
- **SQU** words are often followed by an **A** that says /ah/. **(squad, squall, squat, squash)**

Base	LT's	-s/-es	-ed	-ing	-y/-ly	-er	-est
squad		squads					
squall	all	squalls	squalled	squalling			
square	are	squares	squared	squaring	squarely		
squash	sh	squashes	squashed	squashing	squashy	squashier	squashiest
squat		squats	squatted	squatting		squatter	
squaw	aw	squaws					
squawk	aw	squawks	squawked	squawking			
squeak	ea	squeaks	squeaked	squeaking	squeaky	squeakier	squeakiest
squeal	ea	squeals	squealed	squealing		squealer	
squid		squids					
squint	nt	squints	squinted	squinting		squinter	
squire	ire	squires	squired	squiring			
squirm	ir	squirms	squirmed	squirming	squirmy	squirmier	squirmiest
squirt	ir	squirts	squirted	squirting			
squish	sh	squishes	squished	squishing	squishy	squishier	squishiest

Compound

Base	LT's	-s/-es	-ed	-ing	-y/-ly	-er	-est
foursquare	our are						
pipsqueak	ea	pipsqueaks					

str

/str/ in string

Position: Beginning

Vocalization: Voiced

Classification: Three-letter blend

Group: Trigraph

Multiple spellings (common) /str/: <u>Only STR</u>

Multiple sounds for STR: <u>Only /str/</u>

- **STR** is a three-letter blend. The **S**, **T**, and **R** all retain their original sounds.

Base	LT's	-s/-es	-ed	-ing	-y/-ly	-er/-or	-est
strain	ai	strains	strained	straining		strainer	
strand	nd	strands	stranded	stranding			
strange	ang g(e)				strangely	stranger	strangest
strap		straps	strapped	strapping			
straw	aw	straws					
stray	ay	strays	strayed	straying			
streak	ea	streaks	streaked	streaking	streaky	streakier	streakiest
stream	ea	streams	streamed	streaming		streamer	
street	ee	streets					
strep							
stress	ss	stresses	stressed	stressing		stressor	
stretch	tch	stretches	stretched	stretching	stretchy	stretcher	
strew	ew	strews	strewed	strewing			
strict	ct				strictly	stricter	strictest
stride	i-e	strides		striding		strider	
strife	i-e						
strike	i-e	strikes		striking		striker	
strip		strips	stripped	stripping			
stripe	i-e	stripes	striped	striping	stripy	stripier	stripiest
strive	i-e	strives	strived	striving			
strobe	o-e	strobes	strobed	strobing			

60

Base	LT's	-s/-es	-ed	-ing	-y/-ly	-er	-est
strode	o-e						
stroke	o-e	strokes	stroked	stroking			
stroll	oll	strolls	strolled	strolling		stroller	
strong	ong				strongly	stronger	strongest
strove	o-e						
struck	ck						
strum		strums	strummed	strumming		strummer	
strung	u						
strut		struts	strutted	strutting			

Compound

Base	LT's	s/es	-ed	ing
airstrip	air	airstrips		
backstroke	ck o-e	backstrokes		
bloodstream	oo ea bl	bloodstreams		
brushstroke	sh o-e br	brushstrokes		
chinstrap	ch	chinstraps		
downstream	ow ea			
drawstring	aw ing dr	drawstrings		
hamstring	ing	hamstrings		
headstrong	ea ong			
heatstroke	ea o-e			
keystroke	ey o-e	keystrokes		
mainstream	ai ea			
pinstripe	i-e	pinstripes		
seamstress	ea ss	seamstresses		
shoestring	oe* ing	shoestrings		
songstress	ong ss			
starstruck	ar ck			
streamline	ea i-e	streamlines	streamlined	streamlining
streetcar	ee ar	streetcars		
streetlamp	ee mp	streetlamps		
streetlight	ee ight	streetlights		
streetwise	ee i-e			
strongbox	ong	strongboxes		
stronghold	ong old	strongholds		
strongman	ong			
sunstroke	o-e			
upstream	ea			
watchstrap	wa tch	watchstraps		

<u>thr</u>

/thr/ in throw

Position: Beginning

Vocalization: Voiced

Classification: Trigraph or Digraph Blend

Group: Trigraph

Multiple spellings (rare) /thr/: <u>Only THR</u>

Multiple sounds for THR: <u>Only /thr/</u>

- **THR** is a trigraph. The digraph **TH** is combined with the letter **R.** Some programs may refer to it as a Digraph Blend.

Base	LT's	-s/-es	-ed	-ing	-y/-ly	-er	-est
thrash	sh	thrashes	thrashed	thrashing		thrasher	
thread	ea	threads	threaded	threading		threader	
threat	ea	threats					
three	ee						
thresh	sh	threshes	threshed	threshing		thresher	
threw	ew						
thrift	ft				thrifty	*thriftier*	*thriftiest*
thrill	ll	thrills	thrilled	thrilling		thriller	
thrive	i-e	thrives	thrived	thriving			
throat	oa	throats			throaty	*throatier*	*throatiest*
throb		throbs	throbbed	throbbing			
throne	o-e	thrones					
through	ough						
throw	ow	throws		throwing		thrower	
thrush	sh	thrushes					

See next page for compound words.

Compound

Base	LT's	-s/-es	-ed	-ing
cutthroat	oa			
overthrow	er ow	overthrows		overthrowing
spendthrift	sp ft nd	spendthrifts		
throughway	ough ay	throughways		
throwback	ow ck			

End trigraphs
Printable Cards

nch	**<u>nch</u>** anch ench inch onch unch
tch	**<u>tch</u>** atch etch itch otch utch

nch

/nch/ in lunch

Position: End

Vocalization: Voiced

Classification: End Trigraph or Digraph Blend

Group: End Trigraph

Multiple spellings (common) /nch/: <u>Only NCH</u>

Multiple sounds for NCH: <u>Only /nch/</u>

- **NCH** is a combination of the letter **N** and the digraph **CH**. Some programs will refer to this type of Trigraph as a Digraph Blend.
- **NCH** is always found at the end of a word.
- **NCH** at the end of a word always follows a short sound (or **AU**). This is a similar pattern to the Soldier rule, but because the **N** makes a sound, it is not usually categorized with the Soldiers.
- When children speak or listen to a word with **NCH**, sometimes the **N** sound will not be clear to them.
- Words that end in **NCH** create a plural by added **-ES**, instead of **-S** (**bench – benches**).

Base	LT's	-s/-es	-ed	-ing	-y/-ly	-er	-est
bench		benches	benched	benching			
blanch	bl	blanches	blanched	blanching			
Blanche	e* bl						
branch	br	branches	branched	branching			
brunch	br	brunches	brunched	brunching			
bunch		bunches					
cinch	c(i)	cinches	cinched	cinching			
clench	cl	clenches	clenched	clenching			
clinch	cl	clinches	clinched	clinching		clincher	
conch		conches					
crunch	cr	crunches	crunched	crunching	crunchy	*crunchier*	*crunchiest*
drench	dr	drenches	drenched	drenching			

nch

Base	LT's	-s/-es	-ed	-ing	-y/-ly	-er	-est
finch		finches					
flinch	fl	flinches	flinched	flinching			
french**	fr						
French**	fr						
haunch	au	haunches					
hunch		hunches	hunched				
lunch		lunches	lunched	lunching			
munch		munches	munched	munching	munchy	muncher/ munchier	munchiest
pinch		pinches	pinched	pinching		pincher	
punch		punches	punched	punching		puncher	
quench	qu	quenches	quenched	quenching		quencher	
ranch		ranches				rancher	
scrunch	scr	scrunches	scrunched	scrunching	scrunchy		
staunch	st au				staunchly		
stench	st	stenches					
trench	tr	trenches					
winch		winches	winched				
wrench	wr	wrenches	wrenched	wrenching			

The word **French is not capitalized when it refers to a general object, like **french fry** or **french toast**. However, when it refers to the nationality, for example, the **French** people or the **French** language, it would be capitalized.

Compound

Base	LT's	-s/-es	-ed	-ing
benchmark	ar	benchmarks	benchmarked	benchmarking
bullfinch	ull	bullfinches		
goldfinch	old	goldfinches		
henchmen				
hunchback	ck			
keypunch	ey	keypunches	keypunched	keypunching
lunchbox		lunchboxes		
lunchroom	oo	lunchrooms		
lunchtime	i-e	lunchtimes		
linchpin	y	lynchpins		
punchbag		punchbags		
workbench	wor	workbenches		

66

<u>tch</u>

/ch/ in match

Position: End

Vocalization: Unvoiced

Classification: End Trigraph or End Digraph Blend

Group: Soldier or Silent T

Multiple spellings (common) /ch/: CH, <u>TCH</u>

Multiple sounds for TCH: <u>Only /ch/.</u>

- **TCH** follows a short vowel at the end of words. If the vowel preceding the /**ch**/ sound is long, the end /**ch**/ sound is spelled **CH**.
- **TCH** is always found at the end of a root word.
- Although **TCH** adds a **T** onto the **CH**, the only sound that is heard in these words is the /**ch**/, effectively making the **T** silent. This is because the /**t**/ sound is formed in the same place in the mouth as the /**ch**/ sound.
- The Soldier rule tells us that silent **T** acts as a soldier with **CH** to make sure that the vowel stays soft. The other Soldiers combinations are **CK**, and **DGE**. There are very few exceptions to this rule, but those few exceptions are frequently used words, and are often included in red words lists: **much, rich, such, which**.
- Words that end in **TCH** create a plural by added **-ES**, instead of **-S** (**match – matches**).
- Some programs will refer to this type of Trigraph as a Digraph Blend, since it is blending a digraph with another consonant.

See next page for word list.

tch

Base	LT's	-s/-es	-ed	-ing	-y/-ly	-er	-est
batch		batches	batched	batching			
blotch	bl	blotches	blotched	blotching	blotchy	*blotchier*	*blotchiest*
botch		botches	botched	botching			
Butch	U	Butch's					
catch		catches		catching		catcher	
clutch	cl	clutches	clutched	clutching			
crutch	cr	crutches	crutched	crutching			
ditch		ditches	ditched	ditching			
etch		etches	etched	etching		etcher	
fetch		fetches	fetched	fetching			
glitch	gl	glitches	glitched	glitching			
hatch		hatches	hatched	hatching			
hitch		hitches	hitched	hitching			
hutch		hutches					
itch		itches	itched	itching	itchy	*itchier*	*itchiest*
latch		latches	latched	latching			
match		matches	matched	matching			
notch		notches	notched	notching			
patch		patches	patched	patching	patchy	*patchier*	*patchiest*
pitch		pitches	pitched	pitching	pitchy	pitcher/*pitchier*	*pitchiest*
scratch	scr	scratches	scratched	scratching	scratchy	*scratchier*	*scratchiest*
sketch	sk	sketches	sketched	sketching	sketchy	sketcher/*sketchier*	*sketchiest*
snatch	sn	snatches	snatched	snatching		snatcher	
snitch	sn	snitches	snitched	snitching			
splotch	spl	splotches	splotched	splotching	splotchy		
stitch	st	stitches	stitched	stitching		stitcher	
stretch	str	stretches	stretched	stretching	stretchy	stretcher/*stretchier*	*stretchiest*
switch	sw	switches	switched	switching			
thatch	th	thatches	thatched	thatching		Thatcher	
twitch	tw	twitches	twitched	twitching	twitchy	*twitchier*	*twitchiest*
watch	wa	watches	watched	watching		watcher	
witch		witches					
wretch	wr	wretches	wretched				

See next page for Compound words.

tch

Compound

Base	LT's	-s/-es	-ed	-ing	-er
butterscotch	er sc	butterscotches			
catchphrase	ph a-e	catchphrases			
hatchback	ck	hatchbacks			
hatchway	ay	hatchways			
hitchhike	i-e	hitchhikes	hitchhiked	hitchhiking	hitchhiker
hopscotch	sc	hopscotches	hopscotched	hopscotching	
latchkey	ey	latchkeys			
matchbox		matchboxes			
matchstick	st ck	matchsticks			
patchwork	wor	patchworks			
pitchfork	or	pitchforks			
scratchpad	scr	scratchpads			
sketchbook	sk oo	sketchbooks			
stretchmark	str ar	stretchmarks			
switchback	sw -ck	switchbacks			
switchblade	sw bl a-e	switchblades			
watchband	wa nd	watchbands			
watchdog	wa	watchdogs			
watchmen	wa				
watchstrap	wa str	watchstraps			
wristwatch	wr st wa	wristwatches			

Open syllable short words
Printable Cards

See y in my in the sounds of Y section for open vowel -y sounds.

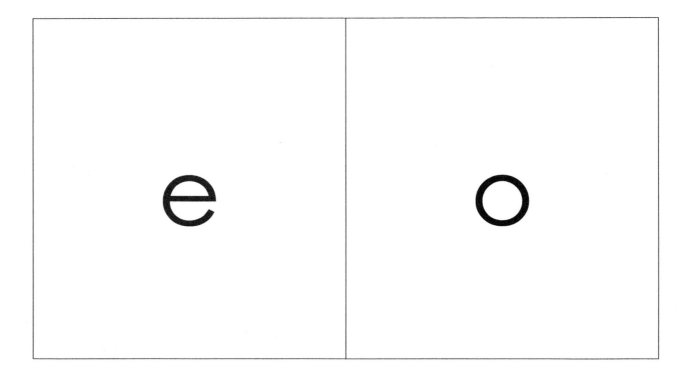

e̱

/ē/ in me

Position: End

Vocalization: Voiced

Classification: Long Vowel

Group: Open syllable

Multiple spellings (common) /ē/: E̱, -Y, EA, EE, -EY, E-E

Multiple spellings (rare) /ē/: IE, EI, -AE

Multiple sounds for E: /ē/ in me, /ĕ/ in hen, /ə/ in happen*
*See jobs of E for more E sounds.

- This list is for one-syllable open vowel words. Multi-syllable open vowels will be included in the Syllables Volume.

Base	LT's	-s/-es/'s	-ed	-ing	-y/-ly	-er	-est
be							
he		he's					
me							
she	sh	she's					
the*	th						
we							
ye							

See next page for compound words list.

Compound

Base	LT's	-s/-es	-ed	-ing	-y/-ly	-er	-est
bebop		bebops	bebopped	bebopping		bebopper	
became	a-e						
*become**	o-e*	becomes		becoming			
befall	all	befalls		befalling			
befell	ll						
began							
beget		begets		begetting			
begot							
begun							
behalf	lf						
behave	a-e	behaves	behaved	behaving			
beheld	ld						
behind	ind						
behold	old	beholds		beholding		beholder	
belay	ay	belays	belayed	belaying			
belong	ong	belongs	belonged	belonging			
below	ow						
bemoan	oa	bemoans	bemoaned	bemoaning			
berate	a-e	berates	berated	berating			
beset		besets		besetting			
beside	i-e	besides					
bestir	ir	bestirs	bestirred	bestirring			
bestow	st ow	bestows	bestowed	bestowing		bestower	
betray	tr ay	betrays	betrayed	betraying		betrayer	
bewail	ai	bewails	bewailed	bewailing			
beware	are						

*The word **the** can be pronounced either /ē/ **(thee)** or /ŭ/ **(thuh)**. When using proper grammar, you say /**thee**/ before words with vowels, and /**thuh**/ before words with consonants. /**thee**/ **acorn**, /**thuh**/ **dog**.

/ō/ in go

Position: End

Vocalization: Voiced

Classification: Long Vowel

Group: Open syllable

Multiple spellings (common) /ō/: <u>O</u>, O-E, OA, OW

Multiple spellings (rare) /ō/: OE, OU*

Multiple sounds for O: <u>/ō/ in go</u>, /ŏ/ in got, /ə/ in button

- This list is for one-syllable open vowel words. Multi-syllable open vowels will be covered in the Syllables Volume.
- There are a few exceptions to the open **O**, but they are very common words, like **two, do**, and **to**. These words will usually be included in red words lists.

Base	LT's	-s/-es	-ed	-ing	-y/-ly	-er	-est
Bo		Bo's					
bro	br						
go		goes		going			
Jo		Jo's					
lo							
Mo		Mo's					
no							
pro	pr	pros					
so							
yo							

Multi-syllable

Open syllables are used extensively in multisyllable words, which will be covered in the syllable volume. The ones listed below are simple versions of the above words.

Base	LT's	-s/-es/'s	-ed	-ing	-y/-ly	-er	-est
Coco		Coco's					
jojo		jojos					
no-no							
so-so							
yo-yo		yo-yos					

Exceptions

Base	LT's	-s/-es/'s	-ed	-ing	-y/-ly	-er	-est
do							
redo							
to							
two							
who		who's					

VCE– Printable Cards

a-e

e-e

i-e

o-e

u-e	y-e

a-e

/ā/ in bake

Position: Split Middle/End

Vocalization: Voiced

Classification: Long Vowel (Split Vowel Digraph)

Group: VCE or Silent E

Multiple spellings (common) /ā/: A, A-E, AI, AY

Multiple spellings (rare) /ā/: EI, EY, EA, EIGH, AE

Multiple sounds for A-E: Only /ā/ in bake

- In the **VCE** pattern, the **E** at the end of the base word causes the vowel to make its long sound.
- The **E** in the **VCE** pattern is sometimes called the "magic e," "silent e," or "bossy e."
- A vowel suffix is a suffix that begins with a vowel (**-ES, -ED, -ING, -ER, -IC, -IST** etc.). When a vowel suffix is added to a **VCE** word, the silent **E** is dropped before the vowel suffix is added. **(skate - skated, bake - baking).**
- When students drop the letter **E** and add **-ED**, they sometimes perceive this as adding just the letter **-D** to the end of a **VCE** word **(bake-baked)**. However, to retain the meaning of the **-ED** suffix, it is important to communicate that the **E** is dropped and **-ED** is added. This also reinforces the pattern of dropping the **E** for adding all vowel suffixes.
- A consonant suffix is a suffix that begins with a consonant (**-S, -LY, -LESS, -FUL, -MENT, -NESS**, etc.). When a consonant suffix is added to a **VCE** words, the silent **E** remains as a part of the root word. It is not dropped, **(bravely, blameless)**.
- **S** says **/s/** as part of **ASE (vase)**. In other **V-SE** combinations, **S** frequently says **/z/**. **ISE-wise, OSE-those,** and **USE-fuse.**
- **VCE plus R**-combinations **(ARE)** are listed in Volume 3 in the R-combinations section. These combinations are listed separately because they are easily confused with R-controlled vowels teams **(ARE-AR)**.
- See **AGE** and **ACE** in volume 3 for more **A-E** words.

a-e

Base	LT's	-s/-es	-ed	-ing	-y/-ly	-er	-est
ate							
bade							
bake		bakes	baked	baking		baker	
bale		bales	baled	baling		baler	
bane							
base		bases	based	basing			
blame	bl	blames	blamed	blaming		blamer	
blaze	bl	blazes	blazed	blazing			
brave	br	braves	braved	braving	bravely	braver	bravest
cage	age	cages	caged	caging			
cake		cakes	caked	caking			
came							
cane		canes	caned	caning			
cape		capes	caped			caper	
case		cases	cased	casing			
cave		caves	caved	caving			
chase	ch	chases	chased	chasing		chaser	
crane	cr	cranes	craned	craning			
crate	cr	crates	crated	crating		crater	
Dale		Dale's					
date		dates	dated	dating			
daze		dazes	dazed	dazing			
drape	dr	drapes	draped	draping		draper	
fade		fades	faded	fading		fader	
fake		fakes	faked	faking		faker	fakest
fame							
fate		fates	fated				
faze		fazes	fazed	fazing			
flame	fl	flames	flamed	flaming			
frame	fr	frames	framed	framing		framer	
gale		gales					
game		games	gamed	gaming	gamely	gamer	
gape		gapes	gaped	gaping			
gate		gates	gated	gating			
gave							
gaze		gazes	gazed	gazing		gazer	
glade	gl	glades					
glaze	gl	glazes	glazed	glazing		glazer	
grade	gr	grades	graded	grading		grader	

Base	LT's		-s/-es	-ed	-ing	-y/-ly	-er	-est
grape	gr		grapes					
grate	gr		grates	grated	grating		grater	
grave	gr		graves			gravely	graver	gravest
graze	gr		grazes	grazed	grazing		grazer	
hate			hates	hated	hating		hater	
Jake			Jake's					
kale								
Kate			Kate's					
knave	kn		knaves					
lake			lakes					
lame						lamely	lamer	lamest
lane			lanes					
late						lately	later	latest
made								
make			makes		making		maker	
male			males					
mane			manes					
mare			mares					
mate			mates	mated	mating			
maze			mazes					
name			names	named	naming			
Nate			Nate's					
page			pages	paged	paging		pager	
pale			pales	paled	paling		paler	palest
pane			panes					
pave			paves	paved	paving		paver	
phrase	ph	a-e	phrases	phrased	phrasing			
plane	pl		planes	planed	planing			
plate	pl		plates	plated	plating			
quake	qu		quakes	quaked	quaking		Quaker	
rake			rakes	raked	raking			
rare						rarely	rarer	rarest
rate			rates	rated	rating		rater	
rave			raves	raved	raving			
raze			razes	razed	razing			
safe			safes			safely	safer	safest
sake			sakes					
sale			sales					
same								
sane						sanely	saner	sanest

Base	LT's	-s/-es	-ed	-ing	-y/-ly	-er	-est
save		saves	saved	saving		saver	
scale	sc	scales	scaled	scaling		scaler	
shade	sh	shades	shaded	shading			
shake	sh	shakes		shaking		shaker	
shale	sh						
shame	sh	shames	shamed	shaming			
shape	sh	shapes	shaped	shaping			
shave	sh	shaves	shaved	shaving		shaver	
skate	sk	skates	skated	skating		skater	
slate	sl	slates	slated	slating			
slave	sl	slaves	slaved	slaving			
snake	sn	snakes	snaked	snaking			
spade	sp	spades	spaded	spading			
spate	sp						
stage	st -ge	stages	staged	staging		stager	
stake	st	stakes	staked	staking			
state	st	states	stated	stating			
stave	st	staves	staved	staving			
take		takes		taking		taker	
tale		tales					
tame		tames	tamed	taming	tamely	tamer	tamest
tape		tapes	taped	taping		taper	
trade	tr	trades	traded	trading		trader	
vale		vales					
vane		vanes					
vase		vases					
wade		wades	waded	wading		wader	
wake		wakes		waking			
wane		wanes	waned	waning			
wave		waves	waved	waving			
whale	wh	whales		whaling		whaler	

Compound

Base	LT's	-s/-es/'s	-ed	-ing	-y/-ly	-er	-est
airbase	air	airbases					
airplane	air pl	airplanes					
baseball	all	baseballs					
baseboard	oar	baseboards					
baseline	i-e	baselines					

Compound, continued

Base	LT's	-s/-es/'s	-ed	-ing
bookcase	oo	bookcases		
briefcase	ie br	briefcases		
cakewalk	alk	cakewalks		
caseload	oa	caseloads		
casework	wor			
cheesecake	ee -se ch	cheesecakes		
clambake	cl	clambakes		
downgrade	ow gr	downgrades	downgraded	downgrading
downscale	ow sc	downscales	downscaled	downscaling
handbrake	nd br	handbrakes		
handshake	sh nd	handshakes		
lakeside	i-e			
lampshade	mp sh	lampshades		
limescale	i-e sc			
makeshift	sh ft			
mandrake	dr	mandrakes		
milkshake	lk sh	milkshakes		
namesake		namesakes		
oatcake	oa	oatcakes		
safeguard	gu ar	safeguards		
salesclerk	cl er -s	salesclerks		
salesroom	-s oo	salesrooms		
shakeup	sh	shakeups		
shortcake	sh or	shortcakes		
shortwave	sh or			
showcase	sh ow	showcases		
slipcase	sl	slipcases		
snakebite	sn i-e	snakebites		
staircase	air st	staircases		
stalemate	st	stalemates		
stargaze	st	stargazes	stargazed	stargazing
suitcase	ui	suitcases		
sunshade	sh	sunshades		
takeoff	ff	takeoffs		
takeout	ou			
telltale	ll a-e			
upscale	sc			
upstate	st			
wavelength	ng th	wavelengths		
wheelbase	wh ee	wheelbases		

e-e

/ē/ in meme

Position: Split Middle/End

Vocalization: Voiced

Classification: Long Vowel (Split Vowel Digraph)

Group: VCE or Silent E

Multiple spellings (common) /ē/: E, -Y, EA, EE, -EY, <u>E-E</u>

Multiple spellings (rare) /ē/: IE, EI, -AE

Multiple sounds for E-E: <u>Only /ē/ in meme.</u>

- In the **VCE** pattern, the **E** at the end of the base word causes the preceding vowel to say its long sound.
- The **E** in the **VCE** pattern is sometimes called the "magic e," "silent e," or "bossy e."
- **E-E** is a rare way to spell the long **/ē/** sound. For middle sounds, **EE** is the most common, followed by **EA**. The long **/ē/** sound at the end of a word is more likely to be **-Y** (**bunny**) or **-EY** (**donkey**).
- A vowel suffix is a suffix that begins with a vowel (**-ES, -ED, -ING, -ER, -IC, -IST** etc.). When a vowel suffix is added to a **VCE** word, the silent **E** is dropped before the vowel suffix is added. (**ceded, scheming**).
- When students drop the letter **E** and add **-ED**, they sometimes perceive this as adding just the letter **-D** to the end of a **VCE** word (**cede – ceded**). However, to retain the meaning of the **-ED** suffix, it is important to communicate that the **E** is dropped and **-ED** is added. This also reinforces the pattern of dropping the **E** for adding all vowel suffixes.
- A consonant suffix is a suffix that begins with a consonant (**-S, -LY, -LESS, -FUL, -MENT, -NESS**, etc.). When a consonant suffix is added to a **VCE** words, the silent **E** remains as a part of the root word. (**merely, genes**).
- **S** says **/z/** as part of the suffix **-ESE** (**legalese, manganese**).

- **VCE plus R-combinations (ERE)** are listed in Volume 3 in the R-combinations section. These combinations are listed separately because they are easily confused with R-controlled vowels teams **(ERE-ER).**
- While **E-E** is not common in single syllable words, the pattern is used extensively in suffixes. At the end of this list are examples of **E-E** in the suffixes **-EDE, -ETE, -ENE,** and **-EME.**

Base	LT's	-s/-es	-ed	-ing	-y/-ly	-er	-est
cede	c(e)	cedes	ceded	ceding			
eke		ekes	eked	eking			
eve							
fete		fetes					
gene	g(e)	genes					
Gene	g(e)	Gene's					
meme		memes					
Pete		Pete's					
scene	sc(e)	scenes					
scheme	sch	schemes					
Steve	st	Steve's					
theme	th	themes					

Compound

Base	LT's	-s/-es	-ed	-ing	-y/-ly	-er	-est
Christmas Eve							
New Year's Eve							

E-E as a part of the suffixes **-ETE, -EME, -ENE, -EDE**

ETE	EME	ENE	EDE
athlete	extreme	acetylene	centipede
compete	morpheme	gangrene	concede
complete			intercede
concrete	phoneme	intervene	millipede
deplete	supreme	kerosene	precede
esthete		reconvene	recede
excrete			secede
obsolete			stampede
secrete			supersede

i-e

/ī/ in bike

Position: Split Middle/End

Vocalization: Voiced

Classification: Long Vowel (Split Vowel Digraph)

Group: VCE or Silent E

Multiple spellings (common) /ī/: I, I-E, Y, IGH

Multiple spellings (rare) /ī/: Y-E, IE, -YE, UY

Multiple sounds for I-E: Only /ī/ in bike

- In the **VCE** pattern, the **E** at the end of the base word causes the vowel to say its long sound.
- The **E** in the **VCE** pattern is sometimes called the "magic e," "silent e," or "bossy e."
- A vowel suffix is a suffix that begins with a vowel (**-ES, -ED, -ING, -ER, -IC, -IST** etc.). When a vowel suffix is added to a **VCE** word, the silent **E** is dropped before the vowel suffix is added. (**bite – biting, like - liking**).
- When students drop the letter **E** and add **-ED**, they sometimes perceive this as adding just the letter **-D** to the end of a **VCE** word **(chide – chided).** However, to retain the meaning of the **-ED** suffix, it is important to communicate that the **E** is dropped and **-ED** is added. This also reinforces the pattern of dropping the **E** for adding all vowel suffixes.
- A consonant suffix is a suffix that begins with a consonant (**-S, -LY, -LESS, -FUL, -MENT, -NESS**, etc.). When a consonant suffix is added to a **VCE** words (**-ly, -s,** etc.) the silent **E** remains as a part of the word. (**finely, bribes**).
- **S** often says **/z/** as part **VCE**. (**ISE-wise, OSE-those, USE-fuse**).

- **VCE plus R**-combinations **(IRE)** are listed in Volume 3 in the **R**-combinations section. These combinations are listed separately because they are easily confused with **R**-controlled vowels teams **(IRE-IR)**.

Base	LT's	-s/-es	-ed	-ing	-y/-ly	-er	-est
bide		bides	bided	biding			
bike		bikes	biked	biking		biker	
bite		bites		biting			
bribe	br	bribes	bribed	bribing			
bride	br	brides					
brine	br	brines				briner	
chide	ch	chides	chided	chiding		chider	
chime	ch	chimes	chimed	chiming			
chive	ch	chives					
cite	c(i)	cites	cited	citing			
crime	cr	crimes					
dime		dimes					
dine		dines	dined	dining		diner	
dive		dives	dived	diving		diver	
drive	dr	drives		driving		driver	
fife		fifes					
fine		fines	fined	fining	finely	finer	finest
five						fiver	
glide	gl	glides	glided	gliding		glider	
grime	gr				grimy	grimier	grimiest
gripe	gr	gripes	griped	griping		griper	
guide	gu	guides	guided	guiding			
hide		hides		hiding		hider	
hike		hikes	hiked	hiking		hiker	
hive		hives					
jibe		jibes	jibed	jibing			
jive		jives	jived	jiving			
kite		kites					
knife	kn	knives					
life		lives					
like		likes	liked	liking			
lime		limes					
line		lines	lined	lining			
Mike		Mike's					
mime		mimes					
mine		mines				miner	

Base	LT's	-s/-es	-ed	-ing	-y/-ly	-er	-est
mite		mites					
nine							
pike		pikes					
pine		pines					
pipe		pipes					
pride	pr						
prime	pr	primes	primed	priming		primer	
prize	pr	prizes	prized	prizing			
ride		rides		riding			
rife							
ripe					ripely	riper	ripest
ripen		ripens	ripened	ripening			
scribe	scr	scribes	scribed	scribing			
shine	sh	shines		shining		shiner	
shrine	shr	shrines					
side		sides	sided	siding			
site		sites					
size		sizes	sized	sizing		sizer	
slide	sl	slides		sliding			
slime	sl				slimy		
smite	sm	smites		smiting			
snide	sn				snidely		
snipe	sn	snipes	sniped	sniping		sniper	
spike	sp	spikes	spiked	spiking		spiker	
spine	sp	spines					
spite	sp						
stride	str	strides		striding		strider	
strife	str						
strike	str	strikes		striking		striker	
stripe	str	stripes	striped	striping		striper	
strive	str	strives	strived	striving		striver	
swine	sw						
swipe	sw	swipes	swiped	swiping		swiper	
thine	th						
thrive	thr	thrives	thrived	thriving			
tide		tides					
time		times	timed	timing		timer	
tribe	tr	tribes					
trike	tr	trikes					
tripe	tr						
trite	tr				tritely		
vibe		vibes					

i-e

Base	LT's	-s/-es	-ed	-ing	-y/-ly	-er	-est
vine		vines					
whine	wh	whines	whined	whining		whiner	
white	wh					whiter	whitest
wide						wider	widest
wife		wives					
wipe		wipes	wiped	wiping		wiper	
write	wr	writes		writing		writer	

Compound

Base	LT's	-s/-es	-ed	-ing	-y/-ly	-er	-est
airstrike	air str	airstrikes					
airtime	air	airtimes					
backside	ck	backsides					
backslide	ck sl	backslides					
bagpipe		bagpipes					
bedside		bedsides					
beehive	ee	beehives					
birdlike	ir						
bloodline	bl oo	bloodlines					
blowpipe	ow bl	blowpipes					
breadline	br ea	breadlines					
campfire	mp	campfires					
chatline	ch						
childlike	ch ild						
coastline	oa st	coastlines					
cowhide	ow	cowhides					
curbside	ur	curbsides					
dateline	a-e						
deadline	ea	deadlines					
dockside	ck	docksides					
downside	ow	downsides					
downsize	ow	downsizes	downsized	downsizing			
downtime	ow	downtimes					
drainpipe	dr ai	drainpipes					
dreamlike	dr ea						
flextime	fl						
goldmine	old	goldmines					
graveside	gr a-e	gravesides					
hairline	air	hairlines					

i-e

Compound, continued

Base	LT's	-s/-es	-ed	-ing	-y/-ly	-er	-est
hayride	ay	hayrides					
hemline		hemlines					
hideout	ou	hideouts					
hillside	ll	hillsides					
hitchhike	tch					hitchhiker	
jawline	aw	jawlines					
joyride	oy	joyrides					
lakeside	a-e	lakesides					
landslide	nd sl	landslides					
lifebelt	lt	lifebelts					
lifeblood	bl oo						
lifeboat	oa	lifeboats					
lifeguard	gu ar	lifeguards					
lifeless	ss				lifelessly		
lifelike							
lifeline		lifelines					
lifelong	ong						
lifespan	sp						
lifetime		lifetimes					
likewise							
limelight	ight						
limescale	sc a-e						
limestone	o-e st						
lunchtime	nch	lunchtimes					
mainline	ai	mainlines					
mealtime	ea	mealtimes					
neckline	ck	necklines					
nightlife	ight						
offline	ff						
offside	ff	offsides					
online							
outline	ou	outlines					
outshine	ou sh	outshines		outshining			
outside	ou						
outsize	ou	outsizes	outsized	outsizing			
oversize	er	oversized	oversized	oversizing			
peacetime	ea -ce						
penknife	kn	penknives					
pinewood	oo						
pinstripe	str	pinstripes					

Compound, continued

Base	LT's	-s/-es	-ed	-ing	-y/-ly	-er	-est
pipeline		pipelines					
playtime	pl ay	playtimes					
rawhide	aw	rawhides					
seaside	ea						
showtime	sh ow	showtimes					
sidearm	ar	sidearms					
sidebar	ar	sidebars					
sidecar	ar	sidecars					
sidekick	ck	sidekicks					
sideline		sidelines					
sideshow	sh ow	sideshows					
sideswipe	sw	sideswipes					
sidewalk	alk	sidewalks					
skyline	y sk	skylines					
snowline	sn ow						
sometime	o-e*	sometimes					
strikeout	str ou	strikeouts					
sunshine	sh				sunshiny		
tailpipe	ai	tailpipes					
teatime	ea	teatimes					
timeless	ss				timelessly		
timepiece	ie -ce	timepieces					
timeshare	are sh	timeshares					
timeworn	wor						
topside		topsides					
treeline	tr ee						
turnpike	ur						
warlike	war						
wayside	ay	waysides					
wildlife	ild						
windpipe	nd	windpipes					
woodbine	oo	woodbines					

o-e

/ō/ in bone

Position: Split Middle/End

Vocalization: Voiced

Classification: Long Vowel (Split Vowel Digraph)

Group: VCE or Silent E

Multiple spellings (common) /ō/: O, <u>O-E</u>, OA, OW

Multiple spellings (rare) /ō/: OE, OU

Multiple sounds for O-E: /ō/ in bone, /ŭ/ in done

- In the **VCE** pattern, the **E** at the end of the base word causes the vowel to make its long sound.
- The **E** in the **VCE** pattern is sometimes called the "magic e," "silent e," or "bossy e."
- **O- E** has a few exceptions where the vowel **O** makes more of short **U** sound. Examples are **done, come, none,** and **some**. These words are often listed in red words lists. This is called the scribal **O**. When scribes were writing words with a lot of up and down strokes (like **n** and **m**), the **U** would be confused with the letters around it. Scribes changed some of the **U**'s to **O**'s, but the short **U** sound was retained. See exception list below the **O-E** word list.
- A vowel suffix is a suffix that begins with a vowel (**-ES, -ED, -ING, -ER, -IC, -IST** etc.). When a vowel suffix is added to a **VCE** word, the silent **E** is dropped before the vowel suffix is added. (**broken, closing**).
- When students drop the letter **E** and add **-ED**, they sometimes see this as adding just the letter **-D** to the end of a **VCE** word (**code-coded**). However, dropping the **E** and adding **-ED** reinforces the pattern of dropping the **E** for adding all vowel suffixes.
- A consonant suffix is a suffix that begins with a consonant (**-S, -LY, -LESS, -FUL, -MENT, -NESS**, etc.). When a consonant suffix is added to a **VCE** words, the silent **E** remains as a part of the root word. (**closeness**).
- **S** often says **/z/** as part **VCE. ISE-wise, OSE-those, USE-fuse.**

o-e

- **VCE** plus **R**-combinations **(ORE)** are listed in Volume 3 in the R-combinations section. These combinations are listed separately because they are easily confused with R-controlled vowels teams **(ORE-OR)**.

Base	LT's	-s/-es	-ed	-ing	-y/-ly	-er	-est
bloke	bl	blokes					
bode		bodes	boded	boding			
bone		bones			bony		
broke	br					broker	
choke	ch	chokes	choked	choking		choker	
chrome	chr						
close	cl	closes	closed	closing		closer	closest
code		codes	coded	coding		coder	
Coke							
cope		copes	coped	coping			
dome		domes	domed	doming			
dose		doses					
dote		dotes	doted	doting			
globe	gl	globes	globed				
gnome	gn	gnomes					
grope	gr	gropes	groped	groping			
hole		holes	holed	holing	holy	*holier*	*holiest*
home		homes					
joke		jokes	joked	joking		joker	
lobe		lobes	lobed	lobing			
lode							
lope		lopes	loped	loping			
mode		modes					
mole		moles					
mope		mopes	moped	moping			
node		nodes					
nope							
note		notes	noted	noting			
owe		owes	owed	owing			
poke		pokes	poked	poking	poky	poker/pokier	*pokiest*
pole		poles					
pope		popes					
Pope							
probe	pr	probes	probed	probing		prober	
quote	qu	quotes	quoted	quoting			
robe		robes					
rode							

o-e

Base	LT's	-s/-es	-ed	-ing	-y/-ly	-er	-est
role		roles					
Rome		Rome's					
rope		ropes	roped	roping			
rote							
scope	sc	scopes	scoped	scoping			
slope	sl	slopes	sloped	sloping			
smoke	sm	smokes	smoked	smoking		smoker	
smote	sm						
sole		soles					
spoke	sp						
stoke	st	stokes	stoked	stoking			
stole	st						
strobe	str	strobes	strobed	strobing			
strode	str						
strove	str						
tome		tomes					
tote		totes	toted	toting			
vole		voles					
vote		votes	voted	voting		voter	
whole	wh				*wholly*		
woke							
wrote	wr						
yoke		yokes	yoked	yoking			

Exception: O-E says /ŭ/ in done

Base	LT's	-s/-es	-ed	-ing	-y/-ly	-er	-est
come		comes		coming			
done							
dove		doves					
love		loves	loved	loving		lover	
none							
shove		shoves	shoved	shoving			
some							

o-e

Compound

Base	LT's	-s/-es	-ed	-ing	-y/-ly	-er	-est
armhole	ar	armholes					
backstroke	ck str	backstrokes					
banknote	ank	banknotes					
beanpole	ea	beanpoles					
drugstore	dr st	drugstores					
earlobe	ear	earlobes					
flagpole	fl	flagpoles					
footnote	oo	footnotes					
forearm	ore ar	forearms					
foxhole		foxholes					
heatstroke	ea str						
keyhole	ey	keyholes					
keynote	ey	keynotes					
keystroke	ey str	keystrokes					
loophole	oo	loopholes					
manhole		manholes					
maypole	ay	maypoles					
molehill	ll	molehills					
notepad		notepads					
overrode	er						
peephole	ee	peepholes					
pinhole		pinholes					
polecat		polecats					
porthole	or	portholes					
slowpoke	sl ow	slowpokes					
smokestack	sm st ck	smokestacks					
sunstroke	str						
tadpole		tadpoles					
wholesale	a-e wh						
wholesome	wh o-e*						
wormhole	wor	wormholes					

u-e

/oo/ in rule

Position: End

Vocalization: Voiced

Classification: Long Vowel (Split Vowel Digraph)

Group: VCE or Silent E

Multiple spellings (common) /ū/ /oo/: U, OO, <u>U-E</u>, EW

Multiple spellings (rare) /ū/ /oo/: UE, OU, EU, UI

Multiple sounds for U-E: <u>/oo/ in rule</u> and /yoo/ in cute

- In the **VCE** pattern, the **E** at the end of the root word causes the vowel to make its long sound.
- The **E** in the **VCE** pattern is sometimes called the "magic e," "silent e," or "bossy e."
- There are two long sounds for **U**. The first says **/yoo/**, as in **cute**. The second says **/oo/,** as in **rule**. This list is for **/oo/** in **rule**.
- A vowel suffix is a suffix that begins with a vowel (**-ES, -ED, -ING, -ER, -IC, -IST** etc.). When a vowel suffix is added to a **VCE** word, the silent **E** is dropped before the vowel suffix is added. (**ruling, tuned**).
- When students drop the letter **E** and add **-ED**, they sometimes perceive this as adding just the letter **-D** to the end of a **VCE** word **(code-coded).** However, to retain the meaning of the **-ED** suffix, it is important to communicate that the **E** is dropped and **-ED** is added. This also reinforces the pattern of dropping the **E** for adding all vowel suffixes.
- A consonant suffix is a suffix that begins with a consonant (**-S, -LY, -LESS, -FUL, -MENT, -NESS**, etc.).When a consonant suffix is added to a **VCE** words, the silent **E** remains as a part of the root word. (**rudely, flutes**).
- **S** often says /**z**/ as part **VCE**. (**ISE-wise, OSE-those, USE-fuse).**

94

u-e

rule

- **VCE** plus **R**-combinations **(URE)** are listed in Volume 3 in the R-combinations section. These combinations are listed separately because they are easily confused with R-controlled vowels teams **(URE-UR)**.

Base	LT's	-s/-es	-ed	-ing	-y/-ly	-er	-est
brute	br						
dude		dudes					
duke		dukes					
dune		dunes					
dupe		dupes	duped	duping			
fluke	fl	flukes					
flute	fl	flutes					
June		June's					
lube		lubes					
lute		lutes	luted	luting			
nuke		nukes	nuked	nuking			
plume	pl	plumes	plumed	pluming			
prude	pr	prudes					
rube							
rude					rudely	ruder	rudest
rule		rules	ruled	ruling		ruler	
rune		runes					
ruse		ruses					
spruce	spr	spruces					
truce	tr	truces					
tube		tubes					
tune		tunes	tuned	tuning			

Compound

Base	LT's	-s/-es	-ed	-ing	-y/-ly	-er	-est
archduke	ar ch	archdukes					
dukedom		dukedoms					
tuneless	ss				tunelessly		

u-e
/yoo/ in cute

Position: Split Middle/End

Vocalization: Voiced

Classification: Long Vowel (Split Vowel Digraph)

Group: VCE or Silent E

Multiple spellings (common) /ū/ /yoo/: U, U-E, EW

Multiple spellings (rare) /ū/ /yoo/: UE, EU

Multiple sounds for U-E: /oo/ in rule and /yoo/ in cute

- In the **VCE** pattern, the **E** at the end of the root word causes the vowel to make its long sound.
- The **E** in the **VCE** pattern is sometimes called the "magic e," "silent e," or "bossy e."
- There are two long sounds for **U**. The first says **/yoo/**, as in **cute**. The second says **/oo/**, as in **flute**. This list is for **/yoo/** in **cute**.
- A vowel suffix is a suffix that begins with a vowel (**-ES, -ED, -ING, -ER, -IC, -IST** etc.). When a vowel suffix is added to a **VCE** word, the silent **E** is dropped before the vowel suffix is added. (**cured, using**).
- When students drop the letter **E** and add **-ED**, they sometimes perceive this as adding just the letter **-D** to the end of a **VCE** word (**use, used**). However, to retain the meaning of the **-ED** suffix, it is important to communicate that the **E** is dropped and **-ED** is added. This also reinforces the pattern of dropping the **E** for adding all vowel suffixes.
- A consonant suffix is a suffix that begins with a consonant (**-S, -LY, -LESS, -FUL, -MENT, -NESS**, etc.).When a consonant suffix is added to a **VCE** words, the silent **E** remains as a part of the root word. (**purely, tuneless**).
- **S** often says **/z/** as part **VCE**. (**ISE-wise, OSE-those, USE-fuse**).

u-e

cute

- **VCE** plus **R**-combinations **(URE)** are listed in Volume 3 in the **R**-combinations section. These combinations are listed separately because they are easily confused with **R**-controlled vowels teams **(URE-UR)**. **UCE** combinations are in the soft **C** section of Volume 3.

Base	LT's	-s/-es	-ed	-ing	-y/-ly	-er	-est
chute	ch	chutes					
cube		cubes	cubed	cubing			
cute						cuter	cutest
fume		fumes	fumed	fuming			
fuse		fuses	fused	fusing			
mule		mules					
muse		muses	mused	musing			
mute					mutely		
puke		pukes	puked	puking			
use		uses	used	using		user	

Compound Words

Base	LT's	-s/-es	-ed	-ing	-y/-ly	-er	-est
jukebox		jukeboxes					

y-e

/ ī / in type

Position: Split Middle/End

Vocalization: Voiced

Classification: Long Vowel (Split Vowel Digraph), Y as a vowel

Group: VCE or Silent E

Multiple spellings (common) / ī /: I, I-E, Y, IGH

Multiple spellings (rare) / ī /: Y-E, IE, -YE, UY

Multiple sounds for Y-E: Only / ī / in type.

- In the **VCE** pattern, the **E** at the end of the base word causes the vowel to make its long sound.
- The **E** in the **VCE** pattern is sometimes called the "magic e," "silent e," or "bossy e."
- **Y** has several different sounds. In the **VCE** pattern, **Y** is considered a vowel and makes the long **I** sound **(type)**.
- A vowel suffix is a suffix that begins with a vowel (**-ES, -ED, -ING, -ER, -IC, -IST** etc.). When a vowel suffix is added to a **VCE** word, the silent **E** is dropped before the vowel suffix is added. **(typing, rhymed)**.
- When students drop the letter **E** and add **-ED**, they sometimes see this as adding just the letter **-D** to the end of a **VCE** word **(type, typed)**. However, to retain the meaning of the **-ED** suffix, it is important to communicate that the **E** is dropped and **-ED** is added. This also reinforces the pattern of dropping the **E** for adding all vowel suffixes.
- A consonant suffix is a suffix that begins with a consonant (**-S, -LY, -LESS, -FUL, -MENT, -NESS**, etc.).When a consonant suffix is added to a **VCE** words, the silent **E** remains as a part of the root word. **(rhymes, hypes)**.
- **VCE** plus **R**-combinations **(YRE)** are listed in Volume 3 in the R-combinations section.

Base	LT's	-s/-es	-ed	-ing	-y/-ly	-er	-est
hype		hypes	hyped	hyping		hyper	
rhyme	rh	rhymes	rhymed	rhyming		rhymer	
style	sy	styles	styled	styling			
thyme	th*						
tyke		tykes					
type		types	typed	typing			

Compound

Base	LT's	-s/-es	-ed	-ing	-y/-ly	-er	-est
typecast	st	typecasts		typecasting			
typeset		typesets					

VE – Printable Cards

ae

ee

ie

-ie

oe

ue

-ye

<u>ae</u>

/ā/ in bae

Position: End

Vocalization: Voiced

Classification: Vowel Digraph

Group: Vowel Team

Multiple spellings (common) /ā/: A, A-E, AI, AY

Multiple spellings (rare) /ā/: EI, EY, EA, EIGH, <u>AE</u>

Multiple sounds for AE: /ā/ in <u>bae</u> and /ē/ in algae

- **AE** is a vowel team. It is similar to **A-E (VCE),** but there is no consonant in between the **A** and **E**.
- In **VE** combinations **(AE, EE, IE, OE, UE, YE),** the silent **E** makes the preceding vowel long.
- **AE** is rare in one-syllable words, and it is often not taught to beginners. **AE** is used in several multi-syllable words, though, and it does follow the same pattern as other **VE** letter teams.
- **AE** is sometimes used to express a plural in a Latin or Greek word. **alumna** (singular) – **alumnae** (plural), **ameba** (singular) – **amebae** (plural)

Base	LT's	-s/-es	-ed	-ing	-y/-ly	-er	-est
bae**							
brae**	br						
nae**							

Bae is a pop culture word, not an authentic word. However, children are familiar with the word and it's a good example of the **AE** pattern

Brae and **nae** are words that are mostly used in Scottish English. **Brae** is the slope of a hill, and **nae** is the Scottish word for **no**.

See next page for multi-syllable.

ae

bae

Multi-syllable

Base	LT's	-s/-es	-ed	-ing	-y/-ly	-er/-or	-est
aerate	a-e	aerates	aerated	aerating		aerator	
Aesop		Aesop's					
aerie**	ie	aeries					
aerobic	-ic				aerobically		
aerogram	gr	aerograms					
aerosol		aerosols					
alumnae	a-						
amebae	a-						
reggae							
sundae		sundaes					

aerie and alumnae can be pronounced with /ai/, or /ee/, so they appear in both **AE lists. The word **aerie** means bird's nest, or an elevated area.

Alumna is a confusing word. Here are the various spellings: **alumna** (one female graduate), **alumnus** (one male graduate), **alumni** (plural male or mixed male and female graduates), **alumnae** (plural female only graduates). (Grammarly.com)

ae

/ē/ in algae

Position: End

Vocalization: Voiced

Classification: Vowel Digraph

Group: Vowel Team

Multiple spellings (common) /ē/: E, -Y, EA, EE, -EY, E-E

Multiple spellings (rare) /ē/: IE, EI, -AE

Multiple sounds for AE: /ā/ in bae and /ē/ in algae

- **AE** has two sounds, /ā/ in **bae** and /ē/ in **algae**. This list is for /ē/ in **algae**.
- Usually in **VE** combinations **(AE, EE, IE, OE, UE, YE)**, the silent **E** makes the preceding vowel long, following the same pattern as **VCE (A-E, E-E,** etc.) This list is the exception, and the second sound of **AE**, /ē/ in **algae**.
- **AE** that says /ē/ in **algae** is rare, and only found in advanced words. This sound does not need to be taught to beginners, because it can cause unnecessary confusion with the **VE** pattern.
- **AE** is sometimes used to express a plural. **antenna** (singular) – **antennae** (plural), **larva** (singular) – **larvae** (plural), **alga** (singular) – **algae** (plural).

Multi-syllable

Base	LT's	-s/-es	-ed	-ing	-y/-ly	-er	-est
aerie**	ie						
algae**	g(/e/)						
anaemia	i*						
antennae							
Caesar	ar	Caesar's					
fibulae							

ae

algae

Base	LT's	-s/-es	-ed	-ing	-y/-ly	-er	-est
hyaena**	y	hyaenas					
larvae	ar						
novae**							
paean							

Aerie and **alumnae can be pronounced with /ai/, or /ee/, so they appear in both lists.

hyaena is an alternate spelling for **hyena. **Hyaena** and **hyena** can be plural with an -s (hyenas) or without an -s (hyaena).

Novae is the plural of **nova. You can also use **novas** as the plural.

**Paean is a song of praise or triumph.

ee

/ē/ in bee

Position: Middle and End

Vocalization: Voiced

Classification: Vowel Digraph

Group: Vowel Team

Multiple spellings (common) /ē/: E, -Y, EA, <u>EE</u>, -EY, E-E

Multiple spellings (rare) /ē/: IE, EI, -AE

Multiple sounds for EE: <u>Only /ē/ in bee.</u>

- **EE** is a vowel team. It is similar to **E-E (VCE)**, but there is no consonant in between the **E** and **E**.
- In **VE** combinations **(AE, EE, IE, OE, UE, YE)**, the silent **E** makes the preceding vowel long.
- **EE** and **EA** are used as alternates. Both are found in the middle and at the end of words, and either can be used to say the long **/ē/** sound.
- There are no easy rules that tell us when to use **EE** in a word, as opposed to **EA**. Below are some general guidelines for spelling the long **/ē/** sound.

  o **Single syllable words:**
    - **EE** is the most common way to spell the long **/ē/** sound and **EA** is the second most common, but both are used in many words. The spelling **E-E (meme)** is rare.
  o **Multi-syllable words:**
    - The long **/ē/** sound at the end of a multi-syllable word is likely to be **Y (bunny)** or **EY (donkey)**.
    - Long **E** is usually spelled with just a single letter **E** when it ends a syllable **(be-have)**. **E**
    - **EE** and **EA**, are used more often in a multi-syllable word when they are in the middle of a root (they are followed by a consonant), **(greed-y, neat-ness)**.

106

ee

- **EER** combinations are found in Volume 3 in the **R**-combinations section. **EER** is listed separately, because it can easily be confused with **R**-controlled vowel teams (**EER**, **ER**).

Base	LT's	-s/-es/'s	-ed	-ing	-y/-ly	-er	-est
bee		bees					
beef		beefs	beefed	beefing	beefy	*beefier*	*beefiest*
beep		beeps	beeped	beeping		beeper	
beet		beets					
bleed	bl	bleeds		bleeding		bleeder	
bleep	bl	bleeps	bleeped	bleeping			
breech	br ch	breeches	breeched	breeching			
breed	br	breeds		breeding		breeder	
breeze	br -ze	breezes	breezed	breezing	breezy	*breezier*	*breeziest*
cheek	ch	cheeks			cheeky	*cheekier*	*cheekiest*
cheep	ch	cheeps	cheeped	cheeping			
cheese	ch -se	cheeses			cheesy	*cheesier*	*cheesiest*
creed	cr	creeds					
creek	cr	creeks					
creep	cr	creeps		creeping	creepy	creepier	creepiest
Dee		Dee's					
deed		deeds	deeded	deeding			
deem		deems	deemed	deeming			
deep					deeply	deeper	deepest
eek							
eel		eels					
fee		fees					
feet							
flee	fl	flees		fleeing			
fleece	fl -ce	fleeces	fleeced	fleecing	fleecy	*fleecier*	*fleeciest*
fleet	fl	fleets	fleeted	fleeting			
free	fr	frees	freed	freeing	freely	freer	freest
geese	-se						
glee	gl						
greed	gr				greedy	*greedier*	*greediest*
green	gr	greens	greened	greening		greener	greenest
greet	gr	greets	greeted	greeting		greeter	
heed		heeds	heeded	heeding			
heel		heels	heeled	heeling			

Base	LT's	-s/-es/'s	-ed	-ing	-y/-ly	-er	-est
jeer		jeers	jeered	jeering			
keel							
keen					keenly	keener	keenest
keep		keeps		keeping		keeper	
knee	kn	knees	kneed	kneeing			
kneel	kn	kneels	kneeled	kneeling		kneeler	
Lee		Lee's					
leech	ch	leeches	leeched	leeching			
leek		leeks					
meek					meekly	meeker	meekest
meet		meets		meeting			
need		needs	needed	needing	needy	*needier*	*neediest*
pee		pees	peed	peeing			
peek		peeks	peeked	peeking			
peel		peels	peeled	peeling		peeler	
peep		peeps	peeped	peeping		peeper	
preen	pr	preens	preened	preening			
queen	qu	queens					
reed		reeds			reedy	*reedier*	*reediest*
reef		reefs					
reek		reeks	reeked	reeking			
reel		reels	reeled	reeling			
screen	scr	screens	screened	screening		screener	
see		sees		seeing		seer	
seed		seeds	seeded	seeding	seedy	*seedier*	*seediest*
seek		seeks		seeking		seeker	
seem		seems	seemed	seeming			
seen							
seep		seeps	seeped	seeping			
sheen	sh						
sheep	sh						
sheet	sh	sheets	sheeted	sheeting			
sleek	sl				sleekly		
sleep	sl	sleeps		sleeping	sleepy	*sleepier*	*sleepiest*
sleet	sl	sleets	sleeted	sleeting			
sleeve	sl -ve	sleeves					
sneeze	sn -ze	sneezes	sneezed	sneezing	sneezy	*sneezier*	*sneeziest*
speech	sp ch	speeches					
speed	sp	speeds		speeding	speedy	*speedier*	*speediest*
spleen	spl	spleens					
spree	spr	sprees					

ee

Base	LT's	-s/-es/'s	-ed	-ing	-y/-ly	-er	-est
squeeze	squ -ze	squeezes	squeezed	squeezing			
steed	st	steeds					
steel	st	steels	steeled	steeling		Steeler	
steep	st				steeply	steeper	steepest
street	str	streets					
sweep	sw	sweeps		sweeping		sweeper	
sweet	sw	sweets			sweetly	sweeter	sweetest
tee		tees					
teen		teens			teeny	*teenier*	*teeniest*
teeth	th					teether	
thee	th						
three	thr	threes					
tree	tr	trees	treed	treeing			
tweet	tw	tweets	tweeted	tweeting		tweeter	
wee							
weed		weeds	weeded	weeding	weedy		
week		weeks					
weep		weeps					
wheel	wh	wheels	wheeled	wheeling			
wheeze	wh -ze	wheezes	wheezed	wheezing	wheezy	*wheezier*	*wheeziest*

Compound

Base	LT's	-s/-es/'s	-ed	-ing	-y/-ly	-er	-est
airspeed	air sp						
beefsteak	st ea	beefsteaks					
beehive	i-e	beehives					
beeswax	-s						
beetroot	oo	beetroots					
birdseed	ir						
Blackfeet	bl ck						
carefree	are fr						
cartwheel	ar wh	cartwheels					
cheekbone	ch o-e	cheekbones					
cogwheel	wh	cogwheels					
duckweed	ck						
feedback	ck						
feedbag		feedbags					
feelgood	oo						
flywheel	fl y wh	flywheels					

Compound, continued

Base	LT's	-s/-es/'s	-ed	-ing	-y/-ly	-er	-est
fourteen	our						
freebase	a-e fr	freebases	freebased	freebasing			
freehand	nd fr						
freeload	oa fr	freeloads					
freeware	are fr						
godspeed	sp						
heedless	ss				heedlessly		
keepsake	a-e	keepsakes					
kneecap	kn	kneecaps					
newsreel	ew -s	newsreels					
nineteen	i-e						
overseen	er						
overseer	er	overseers					
peephole	o-e	peepholes					
peewee							
pinwheel	wh	pinwheels					
seaweed	ea	seaweeds					
seedbed		seedbeds					
sheepdog	sh	sheepdogs					
shoetree	oe* tr	shoetrees					
speedway	sp ay	speedways					
teepee		teepees					
treeless	ss						
treeline	i-e						
treetop	tr	treetops					
weekday	ay	weekdays					
weekend	nd	weekends					
workweek	wor	workweeks					

ie

/ī/ in pie

Position: End

Vocalization: Voiced

Classification: Vowel Digraph

Group: Vowel Team

Multiple spellings (common) /ī/: I, I-E, Y, IGH

Multiple spellings (rare) /ī/: Y-E, IE, -YE, UY

Multiple sounds for IE: /ī/ in pie and /ē/ in chief and cookie

- In **VE** combinations **(AE, EE, IE, OE, UE, YE)**, the silent **E** makes the preceding vowel long.
- **IE** is a vowel team. It is similar to **I-E (VCE)**, but there is no consonant in between the **I** and **E**.
- **IE** is pronounced two ways, **/ē/** and **/ī/**. In general, **IE** is pronounced **/ī/** at the end of a single-syllable word **(pie)**. **IE** is pronounced **/ē/** in the middle of a word or syllable **(chief)**. Both the **/ē/** and **/ī/** sounds spelled as **IE** are uncommon when used as a part of a root word; however, the **-IE** suffix is used in many multi-syllable words **(cookie)**.
- **Y** and **IE** are used as alternates. **Y** and **IE** both say **/ī/** at the end of a single syllable word **(fly, die)**, and they both say **/ē/** as a suffix at the end of a multi-syllable word **(movie, treaty)**.
- The saying "**I** before **E**, except after **C**, or as sounded as **/ā/**, as in **neighbor** or **weigh**." applies to this letter team.
- **I** and **E** together often occur together when the letter **I** is being used as an alternate for the letter **Y**, **(fly – flies)**. The **IE** that is created in this way is not a true phonogram, but it may be perceived that way, and it makes the same sound. See the lower word list for examples.

ie

pie

- When the suffix **-ING** is added to a word ending in **IE**, The **E** is dropped, and **I** changes to **Y**. This prevents a double **ii** in a word. Words of English origin do not have double **i's** (**lie – lying**) (Fulford, 2012)

Base	LT's	-s/-es	-ed	-ing	-y/-ly	-er/-ar	-est
die		dies	died	dying			
lie		lies	lied	lying		liar	
pie		pies					
tie		ties	tied	tying			
vie		vies	vied	vying			

IE created by changing **Y** to **I**.

Base	LT's	-s/-es	-ed	-ing	-y/-ly	-er	-est
cry	cr	cries	cried	crying		crier	
dry	dr	dries	dried	drying		drier	
pry	pr	plies	plied	plying		pliers	
shy	sh	shies	shied	shying			
try	tr	tries	tried	trying			

ie

/ē/ in chief

Position: Middle

Vocalization: Voiced

Classification: Vowel Digraph

Group: Vowel Team

Multiple spellings (common) /ē/: E, -Y, EA, EE, -EY, E-E

Multiple spellings (rare) /ē/: IE, EI, -AE

Multiple sounds for IE: / ī / in pie and /ē/ in chief and cookie

- In general, in **VE** combinations **(AE, EE, IE, OE, UE, YE)**, the silent **E** makes the preceding vowel long, following the same pattern as **VCE (A-E, E-E**, etc.) **IE** in **chief** (this list) is an exception to this rule.
- **IE** is pronounced two ways, / ī / and /ē/. In general, **IE** is pronounced / ī / at the end of a single syllable word **(pie)**. **IE** is pronounced /ē/ in the middle of a root word or syllable **(chief)**. **IE** as a suffix at the end of multisyllable words also says /ē/ **(chief)**. (See the suffix -**IE** list for those words).
- Both the /ē/ and / ī / sounds spelled as **IE** are uncommon when used as a part of a root word; however, the -**IE** suffix is used in a large number of words **(cookie)**.
- **Y** and **IE** work as alternates. **Y** and **IE** both say / ī / at the end of a single syllable word **(fly, die)**, and they both say /ē/ as a suffix (at the end of a multi-syllable word **(movie, treaty)**. Suffix -**Y** and suffix -**IE** are often used as alternate spellings of the exact same word **(cabby, cabbie)**.
- **IE** also says /**ee**/ in words where **IE** is formed as a part of a suffix -**IER, -IED, -IES**. These suffixes usually occur when **Y** changes to **I**, as a vowel suffix is added to the end of the root word **(busy-busier, party-parties)**. In these cases, **IE** is not a pure phonogram; however, it sounds the same and may be perceived as a phonogram.

ie

chief

- The saying "**I** before **E**, except after **C**, or as sounded as /ā/, as in **neighbor** or **weigh**." applies to this letter team.
- See **-IE** in **cookie** for more **IE** words.

Base	LT's	-s/-es	-ed	-ing	-y/-ly	-er	-est
brie	br						
brief	br	briefs	briefed	briefing	briefly	briefer	briefest
chief	ch	chiefs					
fief		fiefs					
field	ld	fields	fielded	fielding		fielder	
grief	gr						
lien		liens					
piece	-ce	pieces	pieced	piecing		piecer	
pier		piers					
shriek	shr	shrieks	shrieked	shrieking	shrieky		
siege	-ge	sieges	sieged	sieging			
thief	th	thieves	thieved	thieving			
tier		tiers					
wield	ld	wields	wielded	wielding			
yield	ld	yields	yielded	yielding			

/ē/ in cookie

Position: End

Vocalization: Voiced

Classification: Suffix

Group: Vowel Team or Suffix

Multiple spellings (common) /ē/: E, -Y, EA, EE, -EY, E-E

Multiple spellings (rare) /ē/: IE, EI, -AE

Multiple sounds for IE: / ī / in pie and /ē/ in chief and cookie

- IE is pronounced two ways, **/ē/** and **/ ī /**. In general, **IE** is pronounced **/ ī /** at the end of a single-syllable word **(pie)**. **IE** is pronounced **/ē/** in the middle of a word or syllable **(chief)**.   The suffix **-IE** is pronounced **/ē/ (cookie)**.
- Both the **/ē/** and **/ ī /** sounds spelled as **IE** are uncommon when used as a part of a root word, but the **-IE** suffix is used in a large number of words.
- The **-IE** suffix turns a word into a noun. For example, the verb **cook** becomes the noun **cookie**. The word **move** becomes the noun **movie**. Some nouns, like **cab**, become related nouns, like **cabbie**.
- At the end of words, **-IE** is an alternative spelling for **-Y. (cabby, cabbie)**
- **-IE** also says **/ē** in words with the suffixes **-IER, -IED, -IES**. These are not true **IE** phonograms, but they say the same sound and may be perceived as phonograms. These suffixes are produced when **Y** changes to **I**, as a vowel suffix is added to the end of the root word. **(busy-busier, party-parties)**.

See next page for **-IE** words.

-ie

cookie

Multi-syllable

Base	LT's	-s/-es/'s	-ed	-ing	-y/-ly	-er	-est
Archie	ar ch	Archie's					
auntie	au nt	aunties					
bootie	oo	booties					
Charlie	ch ar	Charlie's					
Christie	chr st	Christie's					
collie	ll	collies					
cookie	oo	cookies					
cutie		cuties					
Eddie		Eddie's					
genie	g(e)	genies					
goalie	oa	goalies					
hankie	ank	hankies					
Jamie		Jamie's					
Leslie		Leslie's					
movie		movies					
nightie	ight	nighties					
softie	ft	softies					
sweetie	sw ee	sweeties					
Willie	ll	Willie's					

oe

/ō/ in toe

Position: End

Vocalization: Voiced

Classification: Vowel Digraph

Group: Vowel Team

Multiple spellings (common) /ō/: O, O-E, OA, OW

Multiple spellings (rare) /ō/: OE, OU

Multiple sounds for OE: Only /ō/ in toe

- **OE** is a vowel team. It is similar to **O-E**, but there is no consonant in between the **O** and **E**.
- In most words, the **E** is dropped from words when a vowel suffix (**-ing, -ed**) is added to a word. However, for **OE** words, the silent **E** is not dropped **(hoeing, toed)**. (Fulford, 2012)

Base	LT's	-s/-es	-ed	-ing	-y/-ly	-er	-est
doe		does					
foe		foes					
hoe		hoes	hoed	hoeing			
Joe		Joe's					
Moe		Moe's					
toe		toes	toed	toeing			
woe		woes					

Compound

Base	LT's	-s/-es	-ed	-ing	-y/-ly	-er	-est
backhoe	ck	backhoes					
tiptoe		tiptoes					
toehold	old	toeholds					
toenail	ai	toenails					

<u>u</u>e

/oo/ in blue

Position: End

Vocalization: Voiced

Classification: Vowel Digraph

Group: Vowel Team

Multiple spellings (common) /ū/ /oo/: U, OO, U-E, EW

Multiple spellings (rare) /ū/ /oo/: <u>UE</u>, OU, EU, UI

Multiple sounds for UE: <u>/oo/ in blue</u> and /yoo/ in hue

- **UE** is a vowel team. It is similar to **U-E**, except that there is no consonant between the **U** and the **E**.
- As with other long **U** spellings, **U-E** can say either **/oo/** or **/yoo/**. Some of these variations depend on dialect. This is the list for **/oo/**.

Words with /oo/

Base	LT's	-s/-es	-ed	-ing	-y/-ly	-er	-est
blue	bl						
clue	cl	clues	clued	cluing			
cruel	cr				cruelly	crueler	cruelest
due		dues					
duel		duels	dueled	dueling		dueler	
flue	fl	flues					
glue	gl	glues	glued	gluing	gluey		
gruel	gr					`	
rue		rues	rued	ruing			
sue		sues	sued	suing			
true	tr				truly	truer	truest

118

Multi-syllable 161

Base	LT's	-s/-es	-ed	-ing	-y/-ly	-er	-est
accrue		accrues	accrued	accruing			
avenue**		avenues					
Avenue**							
fluent	fl nt				fluently		
fondue							
pursue	ur	pursues	pursued	pursuing		pursuer	
rueful					ruefully		
subdue		subdues	subdued	subduing			
truest	tr st						
undue					unduly		
untrue	tr						

****Avenue** is spelled with a capital letter when it refers to the name of a specific **avenue (Broadway Avenue)**, and it is not capitalized when it refers to an **avenue** in general **(An avenue is wider than a street).**

Compound

Base	LT's	-s/-es	-ed	-ing	-y/-ly	-er	-est
blue jay	bl ay	Blue Jays					

ue

/yoo/ in hue

Position: End

Vocalization: Voiced

Classification: Vowel Digraph

Group: Vowel Team

Multiple spellings (common) /ū/ /yoo/: U, U-E, EW

Multiple spellings (rare) /ū/ /yoo/: UE, EU

Multiple sounds for UE: /oo/ in blue and /yoo/ in hue

- **UE** is a vowel team. It is similar to **U-E**, except that there is no consonant between the **U** and the **E**.
- As with other long **U** spellings, **U-E** can say either **/oo/** or **/yoo/**. Some of these variations depend on dialect. This list is for **/yoo/**.

Words with /yoo/

Base	LT's	-s/-es	-ed	-ing	-y/-ly	-er	-est
cue		cues	cued	cueing			
hue		hues					
fuel		fuels	fueled	fueling			

See next page for multi-syllable.

ue

hue

Multi-syllable

Base	LT's	-s/-es	-ed	-ing	-y/-ly	-er	-est
argue	ar	argues	argued	arguing			
imbue		imbues	imbued	imbuing			
refuel		refuels	refueled	refueling			
rescue		rescues	rescued	rescuing		rescuer	
revue		revues					
tissue*	ss*	tissues					
value		values	valued	valuing		valuer	
venue							

<u>-ye</u>

/ī/ in bye

Position: End

Vocalization: Voiced

Classification: Vowel Digraph

Group: Vowel Team

Multiple spellings (common) /ī/: I, I-E, Y, IGH

Multiple spellings (rare) /ī/: Y-E, IE, <u>-YE</u>, UY

Multiple sounds for YE: /yĕ/ in yes, <u>/ī/ in bye</u>, /yee/ in the word ye

- **YE** is a vowel team. It is similar to **Y-E (VCE)**, except that there is no consonant between the **Y** and the **E**.
- **YE** as a word is pronounced **/yee/**, so it is important to distinguish between **YE** the word, and **YE** the letter team. It may help to put a line in front of the **YE** (**-YE**), to indicate that it is located at the end of a word.

Base	LT's	-s/-es	-ed	-ing	-y/-ly	-er	-est
aye*	a*	ayes					
bye		byes					
dye		dyes	dyed	dyeing*		dyer	
eye*	e*	eyes	eyed	eying			
rye							
stye	st	styes					

The word **dye** refers to imparting color and the word **die** refers to death. For **dye**, the spellings are **dyes, dyed, dyeing**, and for **die** the spellings are **dies, died, dying**.

Compound

Base	LT's	-s/-es	-ed	-ing	-y/-ly	-er	-est
goodbye	oo						
shuteye*	sh e*						

Vowel Teams
Printable Cards

ea	oa

ea

/ē/ in eat

Position: Beginning, Middle, End

Vocalization: Voiced

Classification: Vowel Digraph

Group: Vowel Team

Multiple spellings (common) /ē/: E, -Y, <u>EA</u>, EE, -EY, E-E

Multiple spellings (rare) /ē/: IE, EI, -AE

Multiple sounds for EA: <u>/ē/ in eat</u>, /ĕ/ in bread, /ā/ in steak

- **EA** has three sounds. Long **/ē/** in **eat** is very common, and most **EA** words say long **/ē/**. Short **/ĕ/** in **bread** is the second most common. Long **/ā/** in **steak** is only found in a small number of words.
- The **EA** spelling is most commonly found in the beginning or middle of words but can sometimes be found at the end of a word, like **pea**.
- There are no easy rules that tell us when to use **EE** in a word, as opposed to **EA**; however, below are some general guidelines for spelling the long **/ē/** sound.

  o **Single syllable words:**
    - **EE** is the most common way to spell the long **/ē/** sound and **EA** is the second most common, but both are used in many words. The spelling **E-E** (**meme**) is rare.
  o **Multi-syllable words:**
    - The long **/ē/** sound at the end of a multi-syllable word is likely to be **Y** (**bunny**) or **EY** (**donkey**).
    - Long **E** is usually spelled with just a single letter **E** when it ends a syllable (**be-have**). **E**
    - **EE** and **EA**, are used more often in a multi-syllable word when they are in the middle of a root (they are followed by a consonant), (**greed-y, neat-ness**).

ea

- The sound of **EA** often changes to short / **ĕ** / when the word's grammar (usage) is changed. **mean – meant, heave-heavy**
- **EAR** combinations are listed in Volume 3, in the **R**-combinations section. **EAR** is listed separately, because it can easily be confused with **R**-controlled vowels **(EAR, ER, AR).**

Base	LT's	-s/-es/'s	-ed	-ing	-y/-ly	-er	-est
beach	ch	beaches	beached	beaching	beachy		
bead		beads	beaded	beading	beady		
beak		beaks				beaker	
beam		beams	beamed	beaming			
bean		beans			beany		
beast	st	beasts					
beat		beats		beating		beater	
bleak	bl				bleakly	bleaker	bleakest
breach	br ch	breaches	breached	breaching			
cease	-se c(e)	ceases	ceased	ceasing			
cheap	ch				cheaply	cheaper	cheapest
cheat	ch	cheats	cheated	cheating		cheater	
clean	cl	cleans	cleaned	cleaning	cleanly	cleaner	cleanest
cleat	cl	cleats					
creak	cr	creaks	creaked	creaking	creaky	creakier	*creakiest*
cream	cr	creams	creamed	creaming	creamy	creamer	
crease	cr -se	creases	creased	creasing			
deal		deals		dealing		dealer	
dean		deans					
Dean		Dean's					
dream	dr	dreams	dreamed	dreaming	dreamy	dreamer	
each	ch						
eagle	gle	eagles					
ease	-se	eases	eased	easing	easy	*easier*	*easiest*
east	st						
East	st					Easter	
eat		eats		eating		eater	
feast	st	feasts	feasted	feasting			
feat		feats					
flea	fl	fleas					
freak	fr	freaks	freaked	freaking	freaky	freakier	*freakiest*

*The word **east** is capitalized only when it refers to the proper name of a region, such as the **Middle East**. When you refer to a general direction, such as "Our house is **east** of Main Street.," the word **east** is not capitalized.

ea

eat

Base	LT's	-s/-es/'s	-ed	-ing	-y/-ly	-er	-est
gleam	gl	gleams	gleamed	gleaming			
glean	gl	gleans	gleaned	gleaning			
heal		heals	healed	healing		healer	
heap		heaps	heaped	heaping			
heat		heats	heated	heating		heater	
heave	-ve	heaves	heaved	heaving			
jean		jeans					
Jean		Jean's					
leach	ch	leaches	leached	leaching			
lead		leads		leading		leader	
leaf		leaves			leafy	*leafier*	*leafiest*
leak		leaks	leaked	leaking	leaky	leaker	
lean		leans	leaned	leaning		leaner	leanest
leap		leaps	leaped	leaping		leaper	
meal		meals			mealy		
mean					meanly	meaner	meanest
meat		meats			meaty	*meatier*	*meatiest*
Neal		Neal's					
neat					neatly	neater	neatest
pea		peas					
peace	-ce						
peach	ch	peaches			peachy	peachier	peachiest
peak		peaks	peaked	peaking			
peal		peals	pealed	pealing			
peat							
plea	pl	pleas					
plead	pl	pleads	pleaded	pleading		pleader	
pleat	pl	pleats	pleated	pleating			
reach	ch	reaches	reached	reaching			
read		reads		reading		reader	
real					really		
ream		reams	reamed	reaming			
reap		reaps	reaped	reaping		reaper	
sea		seas					
seal		seals	sealed	sealing			
seam		seams	seamed	seaming			
seat		seats	seated	seating		seater	
sheaf	sh	sheaves					

ea

eat

Base	LT's	-s/-es/'s	-ed	-ing	-y/-ly	-er	-est
sneak	sn	sneaks	sneaked**	sneaking	sneaky	sneaker/sneakier	sneakiest
speak	sp	speaks		speaking		speaker	
steal	st	steals		stealing			
steam	st	steams	steamed	steaming	steamy	steamer	
tea		teas					
teach	ch	teaches		teaching		teacher	
teak							
teal							
team		teams					
tease	-se	teases	teased	teasing		teaser	
treat	tr	treats	treated	treating			
tweak	tw	tweaks	tweaked	tweaking			
veal							
weak					weakly	weaker	weakest
wean		weans	weaned	weaning			
wheat	wh						
yeast	st	yeasts			yeasty		
zeal							

Both the words **sneaked and **snuck** are appropriate past tense words for **sneak**. Words in this book are organized by suffix endings, and not by verb tense, which is why **sneaked** is listed and **snuck** is not.

See next page for Compound Words.

ea

eat

Compound

Base	LT's	-s/-es/'s	-ed	-ing
beachfront	ch fr nt	beachfronts		
beachhead	ch ea	beachheads		
beanbag		beanbags		
beanpole	o-e	beanpoles		
beansprout	spr ou	beansprouts		
browbeat	br ow	browbeats	browbeaten	browbeating
buckwheat	ck wh			
chickpea	ch ck	chickpeas		
cornmeal	or			
daydream	ay dr	daydreams	daydreamed	daydreaming
downbeat	ow	downbeats		
downstream	ow str			
dreamlike	dr i-e			
drumbeat	dr	drumbeats		
eastward	st war			
eavesdrop	-s dr -ve	eavesdrops	eavesdropped	eavesdropping
fleabite	fl i-e	fleabites		
flyleaf	fl y			
heatproof	pr oo			
leapfrog	fr	leapfrogs		
mealtime	i-e	mealtimes		
meantime	i-e			
meatball	all	meatballs		
meatloaf	oa	meatloaves		
moonbeam	oo	moonbeams		
offbeat	ff			
outreach	ou ch	outreaches		
overeat	er	overeats		overeating
overheat	er	overheats		
proofread	pr oo	proofreads	proofread	proofreading
seabed		seabeds		
seabird	ir	seabirds		
seafloor	fl oor	seafloors		
seafood	oo			
seagull	ll	seagulls		
seahorse	or -se	seahorses		
seamen				
seaplane	pl a-e	seaplanes		

ea

eat

Compound

seaport	or	seaports		
seascape	sc a-e	seascapes		
seashell	sh ll	seashells		
seashore	sh ore	seashores		
seasick	ck			
seaside	i-e			
seaweed	ee	seaweeds		
soybean	oy	soybeans		
spearmint	sp ear nt			
steamboat	st oa	steamboats		
steamship	st sh	steamships		
streamline	str i-e	streamlines	streamlined	streamlining
sunbeam		sunbeams		
teabag		teabags		
teacup		teacups		
teammate	a-e	teammates		
teapot		teapots		
tearoom	oo	tearooms		
teaspoon	sp oo	teaspoons		
tearoom	oo	tearooms		
teaspoon	sp oo	teaspoons		
teatime	i-e	teatimes		
upbeat				
upstream	str			
wheatgerm	wh g(e) er			
whole wheat	wh o-e			

<u>ea</u>

/ĕ/ in bread

Position: Middle

Vocalization: Voiced

Classification: Vowel Digraph

Group: Vowel Team

Multiple spellings (common) /ĕ/: E, <u>EA</u>

Multiple sounds for EA: /ē/ in eat, <u>/ĕ/ in bread</u>, /ā/ in steak

- **EA** has three sounds. Long /ē/ in **eat** is very common, and most **EA** words say long /ē/.   Short /ĕ/ in bread is the second most common. Long /ā/ in **steak** is only found in a small number of words.
- There are no easy rules that tell us when to use each sound for **EA**. If a word is new, students should try long /ē/ first and use context to determine the correct sound for **EA**.
- The sound of **EA** often changes when the word's grammar/usage is changed. **(mean – meant, heave-heavy)**

See next page for word lists.

ea

bread

Base	LT's	-s/-es	-ed	-ing	-y/-ly	-er	-est
bread	br	breads	breaded	breading			
breadth	br th						
breath	br th	breaths					
dead					deadly		
deaf							
death	th	deaths			deathly		
dread	dr	dreads	dreaded	dreading			
head		heads	headed	heading	heady	header	
health	th				healthy	*healthier*	*healthiest*
lead			leaded				
realm		realms					
spread	spr	spreads		spreading		spreader	
stead	st				steady	*steadier*	*steadiest*
sweat	sw	sweats	sweated	sweating	sweaty	*sweatier*	*sweatiest*
thread	thr	threads	threaded	threading		threader	
threat	thr	threats					
tread	tr	treads	treaded	treading			
wealth	th				wealthy	*wealthier*	*wealthiest*
yeah	h						

See next page for compound words.

Compound

Base	LT's	-s/-es	-ed	-ing	-y/-ly	-er	-est
airhead	air	airheads					
bedhead		bedheads					
breadboard	br oar	breadboards					
breadbox	br	breadboxes					
breadcrumb	br cr mb	breadcrumbs					
bulkhead	lk	bulkheads					
deadbolt	olt	deadbolts					
deadline	i-e	deadlines					
deadpan							
farmstead	ar st	farmsteads					
forehead	ore	foreheads					
headache	ch a-e	headaches					
headboard	oar						
headcount	ou nt	headcounts					
headdress	dr ss	headdresses					
headfirst	ir st						
headgear	ear						
headhunt	nt					headhunter	
headlamp	mp	headlamps					
headland	nd	headlands					
headlight	ight	headlights					
headline	i-e	headlines	headlined	headlining		headliner	
headlock	ck	headlocks					
headlong	ong						
headrest	st	headrests					
headroom	oo						
headscarf	sc ar	headscarves					
headstrong	str ong						
healthcare	th are						
hothead							
redhead		redheads					
sweatband	sw nd	sweatbands					
sweatshop	sw sh	sweatshops					
sweatsuit	sw ui	sweatsuits					
treadmill	tr ll	treadmills					
warhead	war	warheads					

<u>ea</u>

/ā/ in steak

Position: Middle

Vocalization: Voiced

Classification: Vowel Digraph

Group: Vowel Team

Multiple spellings (common) /ā/: A, A-E, AI, AY

Multiple spellings (rare) /ā/: EI, EY, <u>EA</u>, EIGH, AE

Multiple sounds for EA: /ē/ in eat, /ĕ/ in bread, <u>/ā/ in steak</u>

- **EA** has three sounds. Long /ē/ in **eat** is very common, and most **EA** words say long /ē/.   Short /ĕ/ in bread is the second most common. Long /ā/ in **steak** is only found in a small number of words.
- The most common sound for **EA** is /ē/ in eat. Short /ĕ/ is mostly found in the middle of a word. In most cases, students will need to use context to determine the correct sound for **EA**.
- Some programs do not teach the /ā/ in steak sound for **EA**, and instead treat it as an exception. While one-syllable **EA** /ā/ words are small in number, those few words are used in a number of compound words.

Base	LT's	-s/-es	-ed	-ing	-y/-ly	-er	-est
break	br	breaks		breaking		breaker	
great	gr				greatly	greater	greatest
steak	st	steaks					
yea							

See next page for compound words.

133

ea

steak

Compound

Base	LT's	-s/-es	-ed	-ing	-y/-ly	-er	-est
beefsteak	ee st	beefsteaks					
breakaway	br a- ay	breakaways					
breakdown	br ow						
breakneck	br ck						
breakout	br ou	breakouts					
breakup	br	breakups					
daybreak	ay br	daybreaks					
firebreak	ire br	firebreaks					
greatcoat	gr oa	greatcoats					
heartbreak	ear* br	heartbreaks				heartbreaker	
jailbreak	ai br	jailbreaks					
outbreak	ou br	outbreaks					
steakhouse	st ou -se	steakhouses					
windbreak	nd br	windbreaks				windbreaker	

oa

/ō/ in boat

Position: Middle

Vocalization: Voiced

Classification: Vowel Digraph

Group: Vowel Team

Multiple spellings (common) /ō/: O, O-E, OA, OW

Multiple spellings (rare) /ō/: OE, OU

Multiple sounds for OA: Only /ō/

- **OA** is used mostly in one-syllable words, although it can be found in roots that have had prefixes and suffixes added.
- **OA** and **OW** are alternates. **OA (oat, boat)** is usually used at the beginning or middle of a word, and **OW (snow)** is used at the end of a word. **OE (toe)** is also used at the end of a few words.
- **OAR** words are in Volume 3.

Base	LT's	-s/-es/'s	-ed	-ing	-y/-ly	-er	-est
boast	st	boasts	boasted	boasting		boaster	
boat		boats	boated	boating		boater	
coal		coals					
coat		coats	coated	coating			
coax		coaxes	coaxed	coaxing		coaxer	
foal		foals					
foam		foams	foamed	foaming	foamy	foamier	*foamiest*
goad		goads	goaded	goading			
goal		goals					
goat		goats					
hoax		hoaxes	hoaxed	hoaxing			
Joan		Joan's					
load		loads	loaded	loading		loader	
loaf		loaves	loafed	loafing		loafer	

oa

Base	LT's	-s/-es	-ed	-ing	-y/-ly	-er	-est
loam							
loan		loans	loaned	loaning		loaner	
moan		moans	moaned	moaning			
moat		moats					
oaf		oafs					
oak		oaks					
road		roads					
Sloan	sl	Sloan's					
soak		soaks	soaked	soaking		soaker	
soap		soaps	soaped	soaping	soapy	soapier	*soapiest*
toad		toads			toady		
whoa	wh						

Compound

Base	LT's	-s/-es/'s	-ed	-ing	-y/-ly	-er	-est
boatyard		boatyards					
busload							
carload		carloads					
caseload		caseloads					
goalpost		goalposts					
lifeboat		lifeboats					
longboat		longboats					
meatloaf							
payload		payloads					
railroad		railroads					
raincoat		raincoats					
roadwork							
rowboat		rowboats					
shipload		shiploads					
showboat							
soapbox		soapboxes					
soapsuds							
tailcoat		tailcoats					
topcoat		topcoats					
truckload		truckloads					
upload		uploads	uploaded	uploading			

OO – Printable Cards

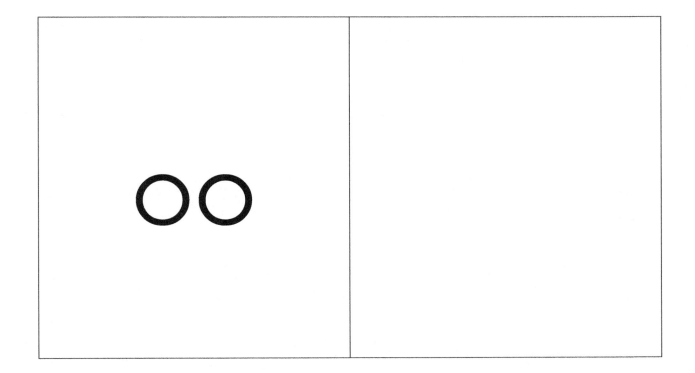

OO
<u>OO</u>

long /oo/ in moon

Position: Middle

Vocalization: Voiced

Classification: Vowel digraph

Group: Vowel Team

Multiple spellings (common) /ū/ /oo/: U, <u>OO</u>, U-E, EW

Multiple spellings (rare) /ū/ /oo/: UE, OU, EU, UI

Multiple sounds for OO: <u>long /oo/ in moon</u>, short /oo/ in book

- OO has two sounds. The first is long **/oo/** in **moon**. The second is short **/oo/** in **book**. This list is long **/oo/** in **moon**.
- The **OO** that says long **/oo/** in moon is the most common sound. The short **/oo/** sound in **book** is uncommon. When students are reading, they should try the long **/oo/** sound first.
- Unlike other long **/oo/** spellings that also say **/yoo/**, **OO** only says **/oo/**, and does not say **/yoo/**.
- **OOR** words are in Volume 3 in the **R**-combinations section. **OOR** is listed separately, because it can easily be confused with **R**-controlled syllables (**OR**, **OOR**)
- Words with "**room**" in them are listed separately, because the **OO** is pronounced differently in different areas of the country. Some people say it more like **/oo/** in **moon**, and some people say it more like **/oo/** in **book**.

Base	LT's	-s/-es	-ed	-ing	-y/-ly	-er	-est
bloom	bl	blooms	bloomed	blooming		bloomer	
boo		boos	booed	booing			
boom		booms	boomed	booming		boomer	
boon		boons					

Base	LT's	-s/-es	-ed	-ing	-y/-ly/-ey	-er	-est
boost	st	boosts	boosted	boosting		booster	
boot		boots	booted	booting			
booth	th	booths					
brooch	br ch	brooches					
choose	ch -se	chooses		choosing	choosy	*choosier*	*choosiest*
coo		coos	cooed	cooing			
cool		cools	cooled	cooling		cooler	
coop		coops					
croon	cr	croons	crooned	crooning		crooner	
doom		dooms	doomed	dooming			
drool	dr	drools	drooled	drooling			
droop	dr	droops	drooped	drooping	droopy		
food							
fool		fools	fooled	fooling			
gloom	gl				gloomy	*gloomier*	*gloomiest*
goo					gooey	*gooier*	*gooiest*
goof		goofs	goofed	goofing	goofy	*goofier*	*goofiest*
goon		goons					
goose	-se		goosed	goosing			
groom	gr	grooms	groomed	grooming		groomer	
groove	gr -ve	grooves	grooved	grooving	groovy	*groovier*	*grooviest*
hoop		hoops	hooped	hooping			
hoot		hoots	hooted	hooting			
loo		loos					
loom		looms	loomed	looming			
loon		loons			loony	*loonier*	*looniest*
loop		loops	looped	looping	loopy	*loopier*	*loopiest*
loose	-se				loosely	looser	loosest
loot		loots	looted	looting			
moo		moos	mooed	mooing			
mooch	ch	mooches	mooched	mooching		moocher	
mood		moods			moody	*moodier*	*moodiest*
moon		moons	mooned	mooning	moony		
moose	-se						
moot							
noon							
ooh		oohs	oohed	oohing			
oomph	ph						
oops	s						
ooze	-ze	oozes	oozed	oozing	oozy		

139

oo

moon

Base	LT's	-s/-es/'s	-ed	-ing	-y/-ly	-er	-est
poo		poos	pooed	pooing			
pooch	ch	pooches					
poof		poofs			poofy	*poofier*	*poofiest*
pooh							
Pooh		Pooh's					
pool		pools	pooled	pooling			
poop		poops	pooped	pooping	poopy	pooper	
proof	pr	proofs	proofed	proofing		proofer	
roof		roofs/rooves	roofed	roofing		roofer	
root		roots	rooted	rooting		rooter	
school	sch	schools	schooled	schooling			
scoop	sc	scoops	scooped	scooping		scooper	
scoot	sc	scoots	scooted	scooting		scooter	
shoo	sh	shoos					
shoot	sh	shoots		shooting		shooter	
sloop	sl	sloops					
smooch	sm ch	smooches	smooched	smooching			
smooth	sm th	smooths	smoothed	smoothing		smoother	smoothest
snoop	sn	snoops	snooped	snooping	Snoopy	snooper	
snooze	sn -ze	snoozes	snoozed	snoozing		snoozer	
soon						sooner	soonest
soothe	th e*	soothes	soothed	soothing			
spoof	sp	spoofs	spoofed	spoofing			
spook	sp						
spool	sp	spools	spooled	spooling			
spoon	sp	spoons	spooned	spooning			
stooge	st -ge	stooges					
stool	st	stools					
stoop	st	stoops	stooped	stooping			
swoon	sw	swoons	swooned	swooning			
swoop	sw	swoops	swooped	swooping			
too							
tool		tools	tooled	tooling			
toot		toots	tooted	tooting		tooter	
tooth	th				toothy	*toothier*	*toothiest*
troop	tr	troops	trooped	trooping		trooper	
whoop	wh	whoops	whooped	whooping		whooper	
whoosh	wh sh	whooshes	whooshed	whooshing			
woo		woos	wooed	wooing			
zoo		zoos					

oo

moon

Compound

Base	LT's	-s/-es	-ed	-ing	-er
afternoon	ft er	afternoons			
bridegroom	br i-e gr	bridegrooms			
carpool	ar	carpools			
childproof	ch ild pr	childproofs	childproofed	childproofing	
darkroom	ar	darkrooms			
doomsayer	ay -s er	doomsayers			
doomsday	ay	doomsdays			
foolproof	pr				
gooseberry	-se err -y	gooseberries			
goosestep	-se st	goosesteps			
heatproof	ea pr				
Liverpool	er				
loophole	o-e	loopholes			
moonbeam	ea	moonbeams			
moonshine	sh i-e	moonshines			
moonstruck	str ck				
offshoot	ff sh	offshoots			
overshoot	er sh	overshoots		overshooting	
poolside	i-e				
preschool	pr sch	preschools			
proofread	pr ea	proofreads		proofreading	proofreader
rainproof	ai pr				
salesroom	a-e -s	salesrooms			
schoolbag	sch	schoolbags			
schoolboy	sch oy	schoolboys			
schoolmate	sch a-e	schoolmates			
schoolwork	sch wor				
seafood	ea				
soundproof	ou nd pr	soundproofs	soundproofed	soundproofing	
tablespoon	ble sp	tablespoons			
taproot		taproots			
teaspoon	sp ea	teaspoons			
toadstool	st oa	toadstools			
tollbooth	oll th	tollbooths			
toothache	th ch a-e	toothaches			
toothbrush	oo br sh	toothbrushes			

Compound, continued

Base	LT's	-s/-es	-ly
toothless	th ss		toothlessly
toothpick	th ck	toothpicks	
whirlpool	wh ir	whirlpools	
wholefood	o-e wh	wholefoods	

"Room" list

Base	LT's	-s/-es	-ed	-ing	-y/-ly	-er	-est
room		rooms	roomed	rooming	roomy	*roomier*	*roomiest*
backroom	ck	backrooms					
ballroom	all	ballrooms					
bathroom	th	bathrooms					
bedroom		bedrooms					
boardroom	oar	boardrooms					
broomstick	br st ck	broomsticks					
classroom	cl ss	classrooms					
cloakroom	cl oa	cloakrooms					
coatroom	oa	coatrooms					
courtroom	our	courtrooms					
darkroom	ar	darkrooms					
guardroom	gu ar	guardrooms					
guestroom	gu st	guestrooms					
headroom	ea						
lunchroom	nch	lunchrooms					
mushroom	sh	mushrooms					
newsroom	ew -s	newsrooms					
playroom	pl ay	playrooms					
restroom	st	restrooms					
roommate	a-e	roommates					
showroom	sh ow	showrooms					
sickroom	ck	sickrooms					
stateroom	st a-e	staterooms					
stockroom	st ck	stockrooms					
tearoom	ea	tearooms					
washroom	wa sh	washrooms					
workroom	wor	workrooms					

OO

short /oo/ in book

Position: Middle

Vocalization: Voiced

Classification: Vowel Digraph

Group: Vowel Team

Multiple spellings (common) short /oo/: OO

Multiple spellings (rare) short /oo/: U

Multiple sounds for OO: long /oo/ in moon, short /oo/ in book

- OO has two sounds. The first is long **/oo/** in **moon**. The second is short **/oo/** in **book**. This list is short **/oo/** in **book**.
- Long **/oo/** in moon is much more common than short **/oo/** in book.
- Words with "**room**" in them are listed as a separate list in the **OO** in **moon** section, because **OO** is pronounced differently in different areas of the country. Some people say it more like **/oo/** in **moon**, and some people say it more like **/oo/** in **book**.
- Exceptions to the **OO** sounds are blood and flood, which both end in **OOD**.

Base	LT's	-s/-es	-ed	-ing	-y/-ly	-er	-est
book		books	booked	booking		booker	
boom		booms	boomed	booming		boomer	
brook	br	brooks	brooked	brooking			
broom	br	brooms					
cook		cooks	cooked	cooking		cooker	
crook	cr	crooks	crooked				
foot			footed	footing		footer	
good		goods			goodly		
hood		hoods	hooded	hooding			
hoof		hoofs/hooves	hoofed	hoofing			

143

oo

book

Base	LT's	-s/-es	-ed	-ing	-y/-ly	-er	-est
hook		hooks	hooked	hooking			
nook		nooks					
roof		roofs/rooves**	roofed	roofing		roofer	
room		rooms	roomed	rooming	roomy	*roomier*	*roomiest*
shook	sh						
soot					sooty	*sootier*	*sootiest*
stood	st						
took							
wood		woods	wooded			woody	*woodier*	*woodiest*
woof		woofs	woofed	woofing		woofer	
wool					wooly	*woolier*	*wooliest*

** **Roofs** is currently the plural for roof in standard English. However, **rooves** is historically correct and will be encountered in some texts. The **F** and **V** are formed in the same part of the mouth and the only difference is that **F** is unvoiced and **V** is voiced. **F** and **V** are frequently used as alternates.

Exception: ood in flood

Base	LT's	-s/-es	-ed	-ing	-y/-ly	-er	-est
blood	bl oo*				bloody		
flood	fl oo*	floods	flooded	flooding			

See next page for Compound Words

oo

book

Compound

Base	LT's	-s/-es	-ed	-ing	-y/-ly	-er	-est
boxwood							
boyhood	oy						
legroom							
sunroof		sunroofs					
woodcut		woodcuts					
bookcase	a-e	bookcases					
bookmark	ar	bookmarks					
bookshop	sh	bookshops					
bookworm	wor	bookworms					
casebook	a-e	casebooks					
cookbook		cookbooks					
cookware	are						
copybook	-y	copybooks					
datebook	a-e	datebooks					
bookplate	pl a-e	bookplates					
bookshelf	sh lf	bookshelves					
bookstall	st all	bookstalls					
bookstore	st ore	bookstores					
brushwood	br sh						
checkbook	ch ck	checkbooks					
childhood	ch ild	childhoods					
footbridge	br dge	footbridges					
redwood							
Redwood							
scrapbook	scr	scrapbooks					
sketchbook	sk tch	sketchbooks					
statehood	st a-e						
storybook	st or -y	storybooks					
withstood	th st						
woodblock	bl ck	woodblocks					
woodchuck	ch ck	woodchucks					
woodpecker	ck er	woodpeckers					

I/Y Alternates
Printable Cards

ai	ay
ei	ey

oi	oy
ui	uy

<u>ai</u>

/ā/ in rain

Position: Beginning or Middle

Vocalization: Voiced

Classification: Vowel Digraph

Group: Vowel Team, I/Y Alternate

Multiple spellings (common) /ā/: A, A-E, <u>AI</u>, AY

Multiple spellings (rare) /ā/: EI, EY, EA, EIGH, -AE

Multiple sounds for AI: <u>Only /ā/ in rain</u>

- **AI** and **AY** are alternatives. The **AI** spelling for **/ā/** is used in the middle of a root word. **AY** is used at the end of a root word. Words of English origin do not end in the letter **I**.
- About twice as many words use **AI** than **AY**.
- **I** and **Y** often work together as "alternates." **Y** combinations (like **AY**) are used at the end of words, whereas **I** combinations (like **AI**) are used in the middle or beginning of words. See the **R**-combinations section of Volume 3 for **AIR** words.

Sound	I – Beginning or Middle		Y - End	
/ā/	**AI**	rain	**AY**	ray
/ē/	**EI**	weird	**EY**	key
/ā/	**EI**	rein	**EY**	hey
/oy/	**OI**	boil	**OY**	boy

ai

Base	LT's	-s/-es/'s	-ed	-ing	-y/-ly	-er	-est
aid		aids	aided	aiding			
aide	e*	aides					
ail		ails	ailed	ailing			
aim		aims	aimed	aiming			
bail		bails	bailed	bailing		bailer	
bait		baits	baited	baiting		baiter	
braid	br	braids	braided	braiding			
braille	br ai ll e*						
chain	ch	chains	chained	chaining			
claim	cl	claims	claimed	claiming		claimer	
drain	dr	drains	drained	draining		drainer	
fail		fails	failed	failing			
faint	nt	faints	fainted	fainting	faintly	fainter	faintest
faith	th	faiths					
Faith	th	Faith's					
flail	fl	flails	flailed	flailing			
frail	fr				frailly	frailer	frailest
Gail		Gail's					
gain		gains	gained	gaining		gainer	
gait		gaits					
grail	gr	grails					
Grail	gr						
grain	gr	grains			grainy	*grainier*	*grainiest*
hail		hails	hailed	hailing			
jail		jails	jailed	jailing		jailer	
laid							
lain							
maid		maids					
mail		mails	mailed	mailing		mailer	
maim		maims	maimed	maiming			
main		mains			mainly		
Maine	ai e*	Maine's					
nail		nails	nailed	nailing		nailer	
paid							
pail		pails					
pain		pains	pained	paining			
paint	nt	paints	painted	painting		painter	
plain	pl	plains			plainly	plainer	plainest
plait	pl	plaits	plaited	plaiting			
praise	pr -se	praises	praised	praising			
quail	qu	quails					

Base	LT's	-s/-s/'s	-ed	-ing	-y/-ly	-er/-or	-est
quaint	qu nt				quaintly	quainter	quaintest
raid		raids	raided	raiding		raider	
rail		rails	railed	railing			
rain		rains	rained	raining			
sail		sails	sailed	sailing			
saint	nt	saints	sainted		saintly		
Saints	nt -s						
slain	sl						
snail	sn	snails					
Spain	sp	Spain's					
sprain	spr	sprains	sprained	spraining			
stain	st	stains	stained	staining			
strain	str	strains	strained	straining		strainer	
strait	str	straits					
tail		tails	tailed	tailing		tailor	
tailor	-or	tailors	tailored	tailoring			
taint	nt	taints	tainted	tainting			
trail	tr	trails	trailed	trailing		trailer	
train	tr	trains	trained	training		trainer	
trait	tr	traits				traitor	
vain					vainly	vainer	vainest
waif		waifs					
wail		wails	wailed	wailing		wailer	
waist	st	waists					
wait		waits	waited	waiting		waiter	
waive	-ve	waives	waived	waiving		waiver	
wraith	wr th	wraiths					

See next page for Compound Words.

Compound

Base	LT's	-s/-es	-ed	-ing	-y/-ly
aimless	ss				aimlessly
bloodstain	bl oo st	bloodstains	bloodstained		
brainless	br ss				brainlessly
brainwave	br a-e	brainwaves			
chainsaw	ch aw	chainsaws			
dovetail	-ve	dovetails	dovetailed	dovetailing	
drainpipe	dr i-e	drainpipes			
hailstone	st o-e	hailstones			
hailstorm	st or	hailstorms			
handmaid	nd	handmaids			
housemaid	ou -se	housemaids			
jailbird	ir	jailbirds			
jailbreak	br ea	jailbreaks			
jailhouse	ou -se	jailhouses			
mailbox		mailboxes			
mailmen					
mainframe	fr a-e	mainframes			
mainland	nd				
mainline	i-e				
mainstream	str ea				
nursemaid	ur -se	nursemaids			
overlaid	er				
overpaid	er				
painless	ss			painlessly	
paintball	nt all	paintballs			
paintbox	nt	paintboxes			
paintbrush	nt br sh	paintbrushes			
pigtail		pigtails			
ponytail	y	ponytails			
railroad	oa	railroads	railroaded	railroading	
railway	ay	railways			
rainbow	ow	rainbows			
raincoat	oa	raincoats			
raindrop	dr	raindrops			

Compound, continued

rainfall	all	rainfalls
rainstorm	st or	rainstorms
sailboat	oa	sailboats
sainthood	nt oo	
shirttail	sh ir	shirttails
tailback	ck	tailbacks
tailbone	o-e	tailbones
tailgate	a-e	tailgates
taillight	ight	taillights
tailpiece	ie -ce	tailpieces
tailpipe	i-e	tailpipes
tailspin	sp	tailspins
tailwind	nd	tailwinds
thumbnail	th mb	thumbnails
toenail	oe	toenails
waistband	ai nd st	waistbands
waistcoat	st oa	waistcoats
waistline	st i-e	waistlines
warpaint	ar nt	
waylaid	ay	

<u>ay</u>

/ā/ in way

Position: End

Vocalization: Voiced

Classification: Vowel Digraph

Group: Vowel Team, I/Y Alternate

Multiple spellings (common) /ā/: A, A-E, AI, <u>AY</u>

Multiple spellings (rare) /ā/: EI, EY, EA, EIGH, -AE

Multiple sounds for AY: <u>Only /ā/</u>

- **AY** is only used at the end of a root word. If the **/ā/** sound is found in the middle of the word, it is usually spelled **AI**.
- About twice as many words are spelled with **AI** than are spelled with **AY**.
- When a suffix is added to a word that ends in **Y**, the **Y** is changed to **I** before the suffix is added (unless the suffix starts with the letter **I**). Usually, if the **Y** is a part of a vowel team, like **AY**, the **Y** does not change to an **I** when the suffix is added, **(play, playing).** However, **AY** is different from other vowel teams, and there are several **AY** words that follow the original rule of changing the **Y** to **I**. **(lay/laid)***
- The **Y** to **I** pattern (discussed in the above bullet point) explains the spelling change of **say+ed** to **said***. In the past, it is likely that the word **said** was pronounced with a long **/ā/**, and that because of the difficulty of that pronunciation, it changed to the more relaxed **/sed/** over time, but it retained its original spelling.
- **I** and **Y** often work together as alternates. **I** combinations (like **AI**) are used at the beginning or middle of root words, and **Y** combinations (like **AY**) are used at the end of root words.

ay

Sound	I – Beginning or Middle		Y - End	
/ā/	**AI**	rain	**AY**	ray
/ē/	**EI**	weird	**EY**	key
/ā/	**EI**	rein	**EY**	hey
/oy/	**OI**	boil	**OY**	boy

Base	LT's	-s/-es/'s	-ed	-ing	-y/-ly	-er/-or	-est
bay		bays					
bray	br	brays	brayed	braying			
clay	cl	clays					
day		days			daily**		
Fay		Fay's					
fray	fr	frays	frayed	fraying			
hay		hays					
jay		jays					
Jay		Jay's					
Kay		Kay's					
lay		lays	laid**	laying		layer	
may						mayor	
May		May's					
nay		nays					
pay		pays	paid**	paying		payer	
ray		rays					
Ray		Ray's					
say		says	*said***	saying		sayer	
Shay	sh	Shay's					
slay	sl	slays	slayed	slaying		slayer	
stay	st	stays	stayed	staying		stayer	
stray	str	strays	strayed	straying			
sway	sw	sways	swayed	swaying			
tray	tr	trays					
way		ways					

Because **AY is a vowel team, in most **AY** words, the **Y** does not change to **I**. However, there are several **AY** words that are exceptions. They *do* change the **Y** to **I**. (**lay/laid**). See note above in the details section to understand the unusual spelling of the word **said**.

ay

Compound

Base	LT's	-s/-es	-ed	-ing	-er
archway	ar ch	archways			
ashtray	sh tr	ashtrays			
beltway	lt	beltways			
birthday	th ir	birthdays			
Blue Jay	ue bl	Blue Jays			
causeway	au -se	causeways			
crayfish	cr sh	crayfishes			
daybreak	br ea				
daycare	are	daycares			
daydream	dr ea	daydreams	daydreamed	daydreaming	daydreamer
daylight	ight				
daytime	i-e				
doomsday	oo s				
doorway	oor	doorways			
downplay	ow pl	downplays			
driveway	i-e dr	driveways			
freeway	fr ee	freeways			
gangway	ang	gangways			
gateway	a-e	gateways			
halfway	alf				
hallway	all	hallways			
hayride	i-e	hayrides			
haystack	st ck	haystacks			
haywire	ire				
hearsay	ear				
heyday	ey	heydays			
highway	igh	highways			
horseplay	pl or -se				
jaywalk	alk	jaywalks			
layoff	ff	layoffs			
mainstay	ai st				
mayday					
mayfly	fl -y	mayflies			
maypole	o-e	maypoles			
midway		midways			
noonday	oo				
outplay	ou pl	outplays	outplayed	outplaying	
pathway	th	pathways			
payback	ck				

Compound, continued

Base	LT's	-s/-es	-ed	-ing	-er
payday		paydays			
payload	oa	payloads			
payoff	ff	payoffs			
payout	ou	payouts			
payroll	oll	payrolls			
playback	pl ck				
playgroup	pl ou gr	playgroups			
playhouse	pl ou -se	playhouses			
playpen	pl	playpens			
playroom	pl oo	playrooms			
railway	ai	railways			
roadway	oa	roadways			
runway		runways			
sickbay	ck	sickbays			
someday	o*				
someway	o*				
speedway	sp ee	speedways			
stingray	st ing	stingrays			
subway		subways			
walkway	alk	walkways			
waylaid	ai				
wayward	war*				
weekday	ee	weekdays			
workday	wor	workdays			

Days of Week

Sunday
Monday
Tuesday
Wednesday
Thursday
Friday
Saturday

ei

/ē/ in weird

Position: Middle

Vocalization: Voiced

Classification: Vowel Digraph

Group: Vowel Team, I/Y Alternate

Multiple spellings (common) /ē/: E, -Y, EA, EE, -EY, E-E

Multiple spellings (rare) /ē/: IE, EI, -AE

Multiple sounds for EI: /ē/ in weird, /ā/ in vein

- EI by itself has two sounds, /ē/ and /ā/. Both are uncommon.
- EI is a part of the letter teams **EIGH** and **EIGHT**.
- There are many ways to spell the long /ē/ sound.   EI is not a common spelling, so students should try the more common spellings first (see the Multiple spellings (common) section above).
- Many **EI** vowel teams are preceded by the soft letter **C (ceiling, deceive, receipt)** Some educators suggest teaching **CEI** as a separate phonogram, instead of teaching the "**I** before **E,** except after **C**" rule, because of the fact that **CEI** is so common, and because the spelling rule poem has so may exceptions.
- **I** and **Y** often work together as "alternates."   **Y** combinations (like **EY**) are used at the end of root words, whereas **I** combinations (like **EI**) are used in the middle or beginning of root words.

157

ei

weird

Sound	I – Beginning or Middle		Y - End	
/ā/	**AI**	rain	**AY**	ray
/ē/	**EI**	weird	**EY**	key
/ā/	**EI**	rein	**EY**	hey
/oy/	**OI**	boil	**OY**	boy

Base	LT's	-s/-es	-ed	-ing	-y/-ly	-er	-est
seize	-ze	seizes	seized	seizing			
sheik	sh	sheiks					
weird			weirded		weirdly	weirder	weirdest

Multi-syllable

Base	LT's	-s/-es/'s	-ed	-ing	-y/-ly	-er	-est
caffeine	-e*						
ceiling	cei ing	ceilings					
conceive	-ve cei	conceives	conceived	conceiving			
deceit	cei	deceits					
deceive	cei -ve	deceives	deceived	deceiving		deceiver	
leisure	u-e s		leisured		leisurely		
protein	pr	proteins					
receipt	cei p	receipts					
receive	cei i-e	receives	received	receiving		receiver	
seizure	ure	seizures					
Sheila	sh a	Sheila's					

158

ei

/ā/ in vein

Position: Middle

Vocalization: Voiced

Classification: Vowel Digraph

Group: Vowel Team, I/Y Alternate

Multiple spellings (common) /ā/: A, A-E, AI, AY

Multiple spellings (rare) /ā/: EI, EY, EA, EIGH, AE

Multiple sounds for EI: /ē/ in weird, /ā/ in vein

- **EI** has two sounds, long **/e/** in **weird**, and long **/a/** in **vein**. Both are uncommon.
- Most of the **EI** say **/ā/** words come from Old French, with the exception of words that are combined with **GH** to make **EIGH**. (The origin of **GH** in **EIGH** comes from Old English).
- **I** and **Y** often work together as "alternates." **Y** combinations (like **EY**) are used at the end of root words, whereas **I** combinations (like **EI**) are used in the middle or beginning of root words.

Sound	I – Beginning or Middle		Y - End	
/ā/	AI	rain	AY	ray
/ē/	EI	weird	EY	key
/ā/	EI	rein	EY	hey
/oy/	OI	boil	OY	boy

- The spelling of **EI** for **/ā/** is rare. Students should try **A, A-E, AI**, and **AY** first.
- Words with **EIGH** (**weight**) are listed in the **EIGH** section of Volume 3.

ei

vein

Base	LT's	-s/-es	-ed	-ing	-y/-ly	-er	-est
beige	-ge						
deign	gn	deigns	deigned	deigning			
feign	gn	feigns	feigned	feigning			
feint	nt						
heir		heirs					
reign	gn	reigns	reigned	reigning			
rein		reins					
skein	sk	skeins					
their	th						
veil		veils	veiled	veiling			
vein		veins	veined	veining			

<u>ey</u>

/ē/ in key

Position: End

Vocalization: Voiced

Classification: Vowel Digraph

Group: Vowel Team, I/Y Alternate

Multiple spellings (common) /ē/: E, -Y, EA, EE, -EY, E-E

Multiple spellings (rare) /ē/: IE, EI, -AE

*-**EY** as a suffix is a common spelling, but EY as a phonogram only includes the word **key**, and compound words that are made from the word **key**.

Multiple sounds for EY: <u>/ē/ in key and honey</u>, /ā/ in they

- The letter team **EY** is pronounced /ee/ and /ā/. This is the list of long /ē/ words.
- I and **Y** often work together as "alternates." **Y** combinations (like **EY**) are used at the end of root words, whereas I combinations (like **EI**) are used in the middle or beginning of root words.

Sound	I – Beginning or Middle		Y - End	
/ā/	**AI**	rain	**AY**	ray
/ē/	**EI**	weird	**EY**	key
/ā/	**EI**	rein	**EY**	hey
/oy/	**OI**	boil	**OY**	boy

- **EY** is much more common as a suffix than it is as a regular letter team.
- See -**EY** in honey for more **EY** words.

See next page for **EY** word lists.17

ey

key/honey

Base	LT's	-s/-es	-ed	-ing	-y/-ly	-er	-est
key		keys	keyed	keying			

Compound

Base	LT's	-s/-es	-ed	-ing	-y/-ly	-er	-est
keyboard	oar	keyboards					
keynote	o-e	keynotes					
keypad		keypads					
keypunch	nch	keypunches	keypunched	keypunching			
keystone	st o-e	keystones					
keystroke	str o-e	keystrokes					
latchkey	tch	latchkeys					
passkey	ss	passkeys					

-ey

/ē/ in honey

Position: End

Vocalization: Voiced

Classification: Suffix

Group: Vowel Team, Suffix

Multiple spellings (common) /ē/: E, -Y, EA, EE, -EY, E-E

Multiple spellings (rare) /ē/: IE, EI, -AE

Multiple sounds for EY: /ē/ in key and honey, /ā/ in they

- The letter team **EY** is pronounced **/ē/** and **/ā/**. As a suffix, **-EY** only says **/ē/**.
- **I** and **Y** often work together as "alternates." **Y** combinations (like **EY**) are used at the end of root words, whereas **I** combinations (like **EI**) are used in the middle or beginning of root words.

Sound	I – Beginning or Middle		Y - End	
/ā/	**AI**	rain	**AY**	ray
/ē/	**EI**	weird	**EY**	key
/ā/	**EI**	rein	**EY**	hey
/oy/	**OI**	boil	**OY**	boy

- **EY** is much more common as a suffix than it is as a regular letter team.
- All suffix **-EY** words are naturally multi-syllable.

-ey

honey

Multi-syllable

Base	LT's	-s/-es/'s	-ed	-ing	-y/-ly	-er	-est
Abbey		Abbey's					
Ainsley	ai sl	Ainsley's					
alley	all*	alleys					
Ashley	sh	Ashley's					
Aubrey	au br	Aubrey's					
Audrey	au dr	Audrey's					
Bailey	ai	Bailey's					
Barney	ar	Barney's					
Bentley	nt	Bentley's					
Bradley	br	Bradley's					
Brittney	br	Brittney's					
Carley	ar	Carley's					
Casey	a-e	Casey's					
Charley	ch ar	Charley's					
Chelsey	ch	Chelsey's					
Chesney	ch	Chesney's					
Corey	or	Corey's					
Courtney	our	Courtney's					
Dewey	ew	Dewey's					
donkey	onk	donkeys					
galley	ll	galleys					
gooey	oo					gooier	gooiest
gulley	ll	gullies					
Harley	ar	Harley's					
Harvey	ar	Harvey's					
Hayley	ay	Hayley's					
honey	o*	honeys					
Humphrey	ph	Humphrey's					
Hurley	ur	Hurley's					
Jeffrey	ff	Jeffrey's					
jersey	er	jerseys					
Joey		Joey's					
Kailey	ai	Kailey's					
Kelsey		Kelsey's					
Kiley	i-e	Kiley's					
Kingsley	ing -s	Kingsley's					
Lacey	a-e	Lacey's					
Laney	a-e	Laney's					

-ey

honey

Multi-syllable, continued

Base	LT's	-s/-es/'s	-ed	-ing	-y/-ly	-er	-est
Langley	ang	Langley's					
Marley	ar	Marley's					
medley		medleys					
money							
monkey	onk*	monkeys	monkeyed	monkeying			
Paisley	ai sl	Paisley's					
Riley	i-e	Riley's					
Rowley	ow	Rowley's					
Ryley	y-e	Ryley's					
Shelley	sh ll	Shelley's					
Shirley	sh ir	Shirley's					
Sidney		Sidney's					
Stanley	st	Stanley's					
turkey	ur	turkeys					
valley	ll	valleys					
Whitney	wh	Whitney's					
Yancey	c(e)	Yancey's					
Zoey		Zoey's					

ey

/ā/ in they

Position: End

Vocalization: Voiced

Classification: Vowel Digraph

Group: Vowel Team, I/Y Alternate

Multiple spellings (common) /ā/: A, A-E, AI, AY

Multiple spellings (rare) /ā/: EI, EY, EA, EIGH, AE

Multiple sounds for EY: /ē/ in key and honey, /ā/ in they

- The phonogram **EY** is pronounced **/ee/** and **/ā/.** This is the list of long **/ā/** words. The **/ā/** sound is rare.
- The **EY** spelling for long **/ā/** is uncommon. Students should try other **/ā/** spellings first, such as **A, A-E, AI,** and **AY.**
- **I** and **Y** often work together as "alternates." **Y** combinations (like **EY**) are used at the end of root words, whereas **I** combinations (like **EI**) are used in the middle or beginning of root words.

Sound	I – Beginning or Middle		Y - End	
/ā/	**AI**	rain	**AY**	ray
/ē/	**EI**	weird	**EY**	key
/ā/	**EI**	rein	**EY**	hey
/oy/	**OI**	boil	**OY**	boy

Base	LT's	-s/-es	-ed	-ing	-y/-ly	-er	-est
grey*	gr	greys	greyed	greying		greyer	
hey							
prey	pr	preys	preyed	preying			
they	th					*their***	
whey	wh						

*****Grey** and **gray** are alternate spellings of the same word. **Grey** tends to be used more in British English and **gray** tends to be used more in American English.

The word **their has an interesting spelling. In general, since the **Y** is a part of a vowel team, it should not be changed to an **I** when adding **-ER**. In the word **their**, the **Y** seems to be changed to an **I**, as is typical of adding a vowel suffix to a word ending in **Y**, but only an **R** is added on to the end of the word, instead of **-ER**. The spelling of **their** may be an attempt to eliminate confusion, as the word would otherwise be spelled "**theier** or **theyer**" The spelling also distinguishes the word **their** from **they're** and **there**. The **EIR** may also be a link to the word's history. According to etymonline.com, the word **they** was originally related to the Old Norse word Þeir, and the word **their** was related to the Old Norse word Þierra. So it is possible that this is not a **Y** turned **I** spelling, and instead is a spelling that reflects the history of the word.

Multi-syllable

Base	LT's	-s/-es	-ed	-ing	-y/-ly	-er/-or	-est
convey		conveys	conveyed	conveying		conveyor	
disobey		disobeys	disobeyed	disobeying			
obey		obeys	obeyed	obeying			
osprey	pr	ospreys					
parley**	ar	parleys	parleyed	parleying			
purvey	ur	purveys	purveyed	purveying			
survey	ur	surveys	surveyed	surveying			

Parley can be pronounced with a long /ā/ or a long /ē/.

OI

/oy/ in boil

Position: Beginning or Middle

Vocalization: Voiced

Classification: Diphthong

Group: Vowel Team, I/Y Alternate

Multiple spellings (common) /oy/: OI, OY

Multiple sounds for OI: Only /oy/ in boil

- The sound **/oy/** is spelled **OY** at the end of root words, and **OI** in the middle of root words.
- **OI** is a diphthong. A diphthong has two vowel sounds that glide from one sound to another. It is different from a digraph, in that a digraph has two vowels that make one new sound, whereas when a person pronounces a diphthong, you can hear two distinct sounds.
- **I** and **Y** often work together as "alternates."   **Y** combinations (like **OY**) are used at the end of root words, whereas **I** combinations (like **OI**) are used in the middle or beginning of root words.

Sound	I – Beginning or Middle		Y - End	
/ā/	**AI**	rain	**AY**	ray
/ē/	**EI**	weird	**EY**	key
/ā/	**EI**	rein	**EY**	hey
/oy/	**OI**	boil	**OY**	boy

168

Base	LT's	-s/-es	-ed	-ing	-y/-ly	-er	-est
boil		boils	boiled	boiling		boiler	
broil	br	broils	broiled	broiling		broiler	
choice	ch -ce	choices				choicer	choicest
coil		coils	coiled	coiling			
coin		coins	coined	coining			
foil		foils	foiled	foiling			
foist	st	foists	foisted	foisting			
groin	gr	groins					
hoist	st	hoists	hoisted	hoisting			
join		joins	joined	joining			
joint	nt	joints	jointed				
joist	st	joists					
loin		loins					
moist	st					moister	moistest
noise	-se	noises			noisy	*noisier*	*noisiest*
oil		oils	oiled	oiling	oily	*oilier*	*oiliest*
oink	-nk	oinks	oinked	oinking			
point	nt	points	pointed	pointing	pointy	*pointier*	*pointiest*
soil		soils	soiled	soiling			
spoil	sp	spoils	spoiled	spoiling		spoiler	
toil		toils	toiled	toiling			
void		voids	voided	voiding			

Compound

Base	LT's	-s/-es	-ed	-ing	-ly
ballpoint	all nt				
checkpoint	ch ck nt	checkpoints			
flashpoint	fl sh nt	flashpoints			
hydrofoil	y dr				
needlepoint	ee dle nt				
noiseless	-se ss				noiselessly
noisemaker	-se a-e -er	noisemakers			
oilskin	sk	oilskins			
pinpoint	nt	pinpoints	pinpointed	pinpointing	
spoilsport	sp or	spoilsports			
tenderloin	er nd	tenderloins			

O̲Y̲

/oy/ in toy

Position: End

Vocalization: Voiced

Classification: Diphthong

Group: Vowel Team, I/Y Alternate

Multiple spellings (common) /oy/: OI, O̲Y̲

Multiple sounds for OY: /oy/ in toy

- The sound **/oy/** is spelled **OY** at the end of root words, and **OI** inside root words.
- **I** and **Y** often work together as "alternates." **Y** combinations (like **OY**) are used at the end of root words, whereas **I** combinations (like **OI**) are used in the middle or beginning of root words.

Sound	I – Beginning or Middle		Y - End	
/ā/	AI	rain	AY	ray
/ē/	EI	weird	EY	key
/ā/	EI	rein	EY	hey
/oy/	OI	boil	OY	boy

Base	LT's	-s/-es	-ed	-ing	-y/-ly	-er	-est
boy		boys					
buoy**		buoys	buoyed	buoying			
coy					coyly		
Floyd	fl	Floyd's					
joy		joys					
Lloyd	ll*	Lloyd's					
ploy	pl	ploys					
soy							
toy		toys	toyed	toying			
Troy	tr	Troy's					

Buoy is pronounced **/boy/** by some people, and **/boo-ey/** by others.

170

oy

Compound

Base	LT's	-s/-es	-ed	-ing	-y/-ly	-er	-est
bellboy	ll	bellboys					
boyfriend	fr *ie** nd	boyfriends					
busboy		busboys					
cowboy	ow	cowboys					
joyride	i-e	joyrides				joyrider	
soybean	ea	soybeans					

Multi-syllable

Base	LT's	-s/-es	-ed	-ing	-y/-ly	-er	-est
ahoy	a-						
alloy	all*	alloys					
annoy		annoyed	annoyed	annoying			
decoy		decoys	decoyed	decoying			
deploy	pl	deploys	deployed	deploying			
employ	pl	employs	employed	employing		employer	
enjoy		enjoys	enjoyed	enjoying			

u̲i̲

/oo/ in fruit

Position: Middle

Vocalization: Voiced

Classification: Vowel Digraph

Group: Vowel Team, I/Y Alternate

Multiple spellings (common) /ū/ /oo/: U, OO, U-E, EW

Multiple spellings (rare) /ū/ /oo/: UE, OU, EU, U̲I̲

Multiple sounds for UI: /oo/ in fruit, / ĭ / in build

- UI is an uncommon spelling for long **U**, both the **/oo/** and **/yoo/** pronunciations.
- I and Y often work together as "alternates." Y combinations (like **UY**) are used at the end of root words, whereas I combinations (like **UI**) are used in the middle or beginning of root words. However, unlike other I/Y alternates that have the same sound, **UI** and **UY** say different sounds.

Sound	I – Middle		Y – End	
/oo/	UI	fruit		
/ ĭ /, / ĭ /	UI	guilt	UY	buy

Base	LT's	-s/-es	-ed	-ing	-y/-ly	-er	-est
bruise	br -se	bruises	bruised	bruising		bruiser	
cruise	cr -se	cruises	cruised	cruising		cruiser	
fruit	fr	fruits	fruited	fruiting	fruity	*fruitier*	*fruitiest*
sluice	sl -ce	sluices	sluiced	sluicing			
suit		suits	suited	suiting		suiter	

ui

fruit

Exception - /yoo/

| juice | -ce | juices | juiced | juicing | juicy | *juicier* | *juiciest* |

Compound

Base	LT's	-s/-es	-ed	-ing	-y/-ly	-er	-est
bodysuit	-y	bodysuits					
fruitcake	fr a-e	fruitcakes					
jumpsuit	mp	jumpsuits					
pantsuit	nt	pantsuits					
snowsuit	sn ow	snowsuits					
suitcase	a-e	suitcases					
swimsuit	sw	swimsuits					

<u>ui</u>

/ ĭ / in build

Position: Middle

Vocalization: Voiced

Classification: Vowel Digraph

Group: Vowel Team, I/Y Alternate

Multiple spellings (common) / ĭ /: I, Y

Multiple spellings (rare) / ĭ /: <u>UI</u>

Multiple sounds for UI: /oo/ in fruit, <u>/ ĭ / in build</u>

-
- The / ĭ / sound of **UI** is rare.
- The **silent U in guilt** is often used in multi-syllable words to indicate the hard sound of **G** or **C** (**biscuit, guilt**). The **U** keeps the **C** and **G** separate from the letter **I**. It is unknown why the letter **B** also follows this pattern **(build).**
- **I** and **Y** often work together as "alternates." **Y** combinations (like **UY**) are used at the end of root words, whereas **I** combinations (like **UI**) are used in the middle or beginning of root words. However, unlike other **I/Y** alternates that have the same sound, **UI** and **UY** say different sounds.
- **UI** usually used as part of one of three combinations: **BUI, GUI,** and **CUI.**

Sound	I – Middle		Y – End	
/oo/	UI	fruit		
/ ĭ /, / ĭ /	UI	guilt	UY	buy

ui

build

Base	LT's	-s/-es	-ed	-ing	-y/-ly	-er	-est
build	ld	builds		building		builder	
built	lt						
guild	ld	guilds					
guilt	lt				guilty	*guiltier*	*guiltiest*

Multi-syllable

Base	LT's	-s/-es	-ed	-ing	-y/-ly	-er	-est
biscuit		biscuits					
circuit	c(i) ir	circuits	circuited	circuiting			
inbuilt	lt						
rebuild	ld	rebuilds		rebuilding			

UY

/ ī / in buy

Position: End

Vocalization: Voiced

Classification: Vowel Digraph

Group: Vowel Team, I/Y Alternate

Multiple spellings (common) / ī /: I, I-E, Y, IGH

Multiple spellings (rare) / ī /: Y-E, IE, YE, UY

Multiple sounds: / ī / in buy

- **UY** in **buy** is used only in two words, **buy** and **guy**. Some educators teach **buy** and **guy** as individual words, instead of teaching **UY** as a phonogram.
- **I** and **Y** often work together as "alternates." **Y** combinations (like **UY**) are used at the end of root words, whereas **I** combinations (like **UI**) are used in the middle or beginning of root words. However, unlike other **I/Y** alternates that have the same sound, **UI** and **UY** say different sounds.

Sound	I – Middle		Y – End	
/oo/	UI	fruit		
/ ĭ /, / ī /	UI	guilt	UY	buy

Base	LT's	-s/-es	-ed	-ing	-y/-ly	-er	-est
buy		buys		buying		buyer	
guy		guys					

var

uy

Multi-syllable

Base	LT's	-s/-es	-ed	-ing	-y/-ly	-er	-est
buyout	ou	buyouts					
wise-guy	i-e	wise-guys					

U/W Alternates
Printable Cards

au | aw

eu | ew

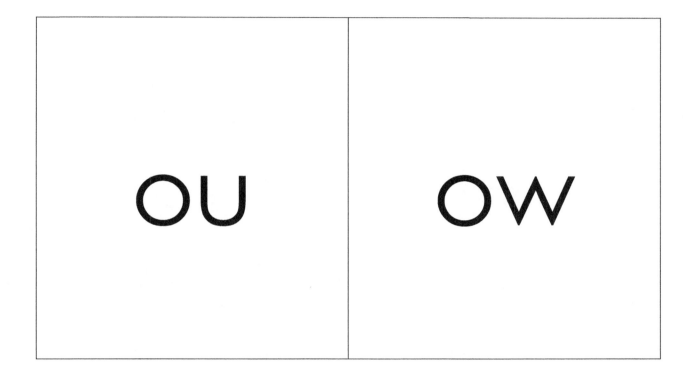

<u>au</u>

/aw/ or /ŏ/ in cause

Position: Middle

Vocalization: Voiced

Classification: /ah/ - Vowel Digraph or /aw/ Diphthong

Group: Vowel Team, U/W Alternate

Multiple spellings (common) /ŏ/ or /aw/: O, AW, <u>AU</u>

Multiple spellings (rare) /ŏ/ or /aw/: AUGH

Multiple sounds for AU: <u>Only /aw/ or /ŏ/ in cause</u>

- **U** and **W** often work together as "alternates." **W** combinations (like **AW**) are used at the end of root words, whereas **U** combinations (like **AU**) are used in the middle or beginning of root words. **AW** is also used as a spelling for **/aw/** in the middle of words only before the letters **N, L,** and **K (AWN** in **lawn, AWL** in **brawl, AWK** in **hawk).**
- **AU** is also a part of the phonogram **AUGHT.**

Sound	U - Beginning or Middle		W -End	
/aw/	**AU**	cause	**AW**	saw
/yoo/	**EU**	feud	**EW**	few
/oo/			**EW**	blew
/ow/	**OU**	couch	**OW**	cow
/ō/	**OU**	soul	**OW**	snow
/oo/	**OU**	soup		
/ŭ/	**OU**	touch		

Base	LT's	-s/-es	-ed	-ing	-y/-ly	-er	-est
auto		autos					
baulk	lk	baulks	baulked	baulking		baulker	
caulk	lk	caulks	caulked	caulking		caulker	
cause	-se	causes	caused	causing			
clause	cl -se	clauses					
daub		daubs	daubed	daubing		dauber	
daunt	nt						
fault	lt	faults	faulted	faulting			
faun		fauns					
fraud	fr	frauds					
gaunt	nt					gaunter	gauntest
gauze	ze						
haul		hauls	hauled	hauling		hauler	
haunt	nt	haunts	haunted	haunting			
jaunt	nt	jaunts	jaunted	jaunting			
laud		lauds	lauded	lauding			
launch	nch	launches	launched	launching		launcher	
maul		mauls	mauled	mauling			
mauve	-ve						
pause	-se	pauses	paused	pausing			
sauce	-ce	sauces	sauced	saucing	saucy	saucer/*saucier*	*sauciest*
taunt	nt	taunts	taunted	taunting			
taut					tautly	tauter	tautest
vault	lt	vaults	vaulted	vaulting			

<u>aw</u>

/aw/ or /ŏ/ in saw

Position: End

Vocalization: Voiced

Classification: /ah/ - Vowel Digraph or /aw/ Diphthong

Group: Vowel Team, U/W Alternate

Multiple spellings (common) /ŏ/ or /aw/: O, AW, AU

Multiple spellings (rare) /ŏ/ or /aw/: AUGH

Multiple sounds for AW: <u>Only /aw/ or /ŏ/ in saw</u>

- In some dialects, **AW** sounds like short /ŏ/. In other dialects, **AW** functions as a diphthong, with two sounds that glide into each other /ahw/
- **AW** is considered a vowel digraph. Some educators consider **W** in **AW** to be a vowel.
- **W** and **U** often work together as "alternates." **W** combinations (like **AW**) are used at the end of root words, whereas **U** combinations (like **AU**) are used in the middle or beginning of root words. **AW** is also used as a spelling for /**aw**/ in the middle of words before ending consonants, mostly the letters **N, L,** and **K (AWN in lawn, AWL in brawl, AWK in hawk).**

See next page for word lists.

aw

Sound	U - Beginning or Middle		W -End	
/aw/	AU	cause	AW	saw
/yoo/	EU	feud	EW	few
/oo/			EW	blew
/ow/	OU	couch	OW	cow
/ō/	OU	soul	OW	snow
/oo/	OU	soup		
/ŭ/	OU	touch		

Base	LT's	-s/-es	-ed	-ing	-y/-ly	-er	-est
bawl		bawls	bawled	bawling		bawler	
brawl	br	brawls	brawled	brawling		brawler	
brawn	br				brawny	*brawnier*	*brawniest*
caw		caws	cawed	cawing			
claw	cl	claws	clawed	clawing			
dawn		dawns	dawned	dawning			
draw	dr	draws		drawing		drawer	
drawl	dr	drawls	drawled	drawling			
fawn		fawns	fawned	fawning			
gawk		gawks	gawked	gawking		gawker	
gnaw	gn	gnaws	gnawed	gnawing		gnawer	
haw							
hawk		hawks					
jaw		jaws	jawed	jawing			
law		laws					
lawn		lawns					
paw		paws	pawed	pawing			
pawn		pawns	pawned	pawning			
prawn	pr	prawns					
raw						rawer	rawest
saw		saws	sawed	sawing			
sawn							
shawl	sh	shawls					
slaw	sl	slaws					
sprawl	spr	sprawls	sprawled	sprawling		sprawler	
squaw	squ	squaws					

Base	LT's	-s/-es	-ed	-ing	-y/-ly	-er	-est
squawk	squ	squawks	squawked	squawking		squawker	
straw	str	straws					
thaw	th	thaws	thawed	thawing			
yawn		yawns	yawned	yawning		yawner	

Compound

Base	LT's	-s/-es	-ed	-ing	-y/-ly	-er	-est
Blackhawks	bl ck -s						
chainsaw	ch ai	chainsaws					
crawfish	cr sh	crawfishes					
drawback	dr ck	drawbacks					
flawless	fl ss				flawlessly		
hawthorn	th or	hawthorns					
jawbone	o-e	jawbones					
jawline	i-e	jawlines					
jigsaw		jigsaws					
lawsuit	ui	lawsuits					
lockjaw	ck						
outlaw	ou	outlaws	outlawed	outlawing			
overdraw	er dr	overdraws		overdrawing		overdrawer	
pawnshop	sh	pawnshops					
pawpaw		pawpaws					
rickshaw	ck sh	rickshaws					
sawdust	st						
sawmill	ll	sawmills					
seesaw	ee	seesaws	seesawed	seesawing			
southpaw	ou th	southpaws					
withdraw	th dr	withdraws		withdrawing		withdrawer	
withdrawn	th dr						

eu

/oo/ in sleuth

Position: Middle

Vocalization: Voiced

Classification: Vowel Digraph

Group: Vowel Team, U/W Alternate

Multiple spellings (common) /ū/ /oo/: U, OO, U-E, EW

Multiple spellings (rare) /ū/ /oo/: UE, OU, EU, UI

Multiple sounds for EU: /oo/ in sleuth, /yoo/ in feud

- The two sounds **/yoo/** and **/oo/** can be spelled **EU** or **EW** (and several other ways – see multiple spellings for these sounds). **EW** is the more common spelling of the two, but both are uncommon.
- **W** and **U** often work together as "alternates."   **W** combinations (like **EW**) are used at the end of root words, whereas **U** combinations (like **EU**) are used in the middle or beginning of root words.

Sound	U - Beginning or Middle		W -End	
/aw/	**AU**	cause	**AW**	saw
/yoo/	**EU**	feud	**EW**	few
/oo/			**EW**	blew
/ow/	**OU**	couch	**OW**	cow
/ō/	**OU**	soul	**OW**	snow
/oo/	**OU**	soup		
/ŭ/	**OU**	touch		

185

eu

sleuth

Base	LT's	-s/-es	-ed	-ing	-y/-ly	-er	-est
deuce	-ce	deuces					
sleuth	sl th	sleuths	sleuthed	sleuthing			

Multi-syllable

Base	LT's	-s/-es	-ed	-ing	-y/-ly	-er	-est
leukemia	i*						
neuter	er	neuters	neutered	neutering			
neutral	tr						
neutron	tr	neutrons					
pseudo	ps						

eu

/yoo/ in feud

Position: Beginning or Middle

Vocalization: Voiced

Classification: Vowel Digraph

Group: Vowel Team, U/W Alternate

Multiple spellings (common) /ū/ /yoo/: U, U-E, EW

Multiple spellings (rare) /ū/ /yoo/: UE, EU

Multiple sounds for EU: /oo/ in sleuth, /yoo/ in feud

- The two sounds **/yoo/** and **/oo/** can be spelled **EU** or **EW** (and several other ways – see multiple spellings for these sounds). **EW** is the more common spelling of the two, but both are uncommon.
- **W** and **U** often work together as "alternates." **W** combinations (like **EW**) are used at the end of root words, whereas **U** combinations (like **EU**) are used in the middle or beginning of root words.

Sound	U - Beginning or Middle		W -End	
/aw/	**AU**	cause	**AW**	saw
/yoo/	**EU**	feud	**EW**	few
/oo/			**EW**	blew
/ow/	**OU**	couch	**OW**	cow
/ō/	**OU**	soul	**OW**	snow
/oo/	**OU**	soup		
/ŭ/	**OU**	touch		

187

eu

feud

Base	LT's	-s/-es	-ed	-ing	-y/-ly	-er	-est
feud		feuds	feuded	feuding			

Multi-syllable

Base	LT's	-s/-es/'s	-ed	-ing	-y/-ly	-er	-est
euphoria	ph or i*						
feudal							

EUR /yer/*

Base	LT's	-s/-es	-ed	-ing	-y/-ly	-er	-est
euro		euros					
eureka							
Europe	o-e	Europe's					

*Words with EUR may sound more like /yer/

ew

/oo/ in blew

Position: End

Vocalization: Voiced

Classification: Vowel Digraph

Group: Vowel Team, U/W Alternate

Multiple spellings (common) /ū/ /oo/: U, OO, U-E, <u>EW</u>

Multiple spellings (rare) /ū/ /oo/: UE, OU, EU, UI

Multiple sounds for EW: <u>/oo/ in blew</u>, /yoo/ in few

- In the **EW** phonogram, some educators consider **W** is considered to be a vowel.
- **EW** is pronounced in two ways, **/yoo/** and **/oo/.** This list is the **/oo/** list.
- **W** and **U** often work together as "alternates."   **W** combinations (like **EW**) are used at the end of root words, whereas **U** combinations (like **EU**) are used in the middle or beginning of root words.

Sound	U - Beginning or Middle		W -End	
/aw/	**AU**	cause	**AW**	saw
/yoo/	**EU**	feud	**EW**	few
/oo/			**EW**	blew
/ow/	**OU**	couch	**OW**	cow
/ō/	**OU**	soul	**OW**	snow
/oo/	**OU**	soup		
/ŭ/	**OU**	touch		

ew

Base	LT's	-s/-es/'s	-ed	-ing	-y/-ly	-er	-est
blew	bl						
chew**	ch	chews	chewed	chewing	chewy	*chewier*	*chewiest*
crew	cr	crews	crewed	crewing			
drew	dr						
Drew	dr	Drew's					
flew	fl						
grew	gr						
knew	kn						
new		news			newly	newer	newest
newt		newts					
Newt		Newt's					
screw	scr	screws	screwed	screwing	screwy	*screwier*	*screwiest*
shrew	shr	shrews					
slew	sl						
stew	st	stews	stewed	stewing		stewer	
strew	str						
threw	thr						
whew	wh						

** In some dialects, the **EW** in **chew** says **/yoo/**.

Compound

Base	LT's	-s/-es	-ed	-ing	-y/-ly	-er	-est
aircrew	air cr	aircrews					
corkscrew	or scr	corkscrews					
crewmen	cr						
dewdrop	dr	dewdrops					
newborn	or	newborns					
newscast	st -s	newscasts					
newsflash	fl sh -s	newsflashes					
newsletter	ew -er -s	newsletters					
newsprint	pr nt -s	newsprints					
newsreel	ee -s	newsreels					
newsroom	oo -s	newsrooms					
newsstand	st nd	newsstands					
overthrew	er thr						

Exception

Base	LT's	-s/-es/'s	-ed	-ing	-y/-ly	-er	-est
sew		sews	sewed	sewing			
sewn							

ew

/yoo/ in few

Position: End

Vocalization: Voiced

Classification: Vowel Digraph

Group: Vowel Team, U/W Alternate

Multiple spellings (common) /ū/ /yoo/: U, U-E, <u>EW</u>

Multiple spellings (rare) /ū/ /yoo/: UE, EU

Multiple sounds for EW: /oo/ in blew, <u>/yoo/ in few</u>

- In the **EW** phonogram, some educators consider **W** to be a vowel.
- **EW** is pronounced in two ways, **/yoo/** and **/oo/.** This list is the **/yoo/** list.
- **EW** is an uncommon spelling, so students should try other **/yoo/** spellings first.
- **W** and **U** often work together as "alternates."   **W** combinations (like **EW**) are used at the end of root words, whereas **U** combinations (like **EU**) are used in the middle or beginning of root words.

Sound	U - Beginning or Middle		W -End	
/aw/	**AU**	cause	**AW**	saw
/yoo/	**EU**	feud	**EW**	few
/oo/			**EW**	blew
/ow/	**OU**	couch	**OW**	cow
/ō/	**OU**	soul	**OW**	snow
/oo/	**OU**	soup		
/ŭ/	**OU**	touch		

ew

few

Base	LT's	-s/-es	-ed	-ing	-y/-ly	-er	-est
chew		chews	chewed	chewing	chewy	*chewier*	*chewiest*
few						fewer	fewest
hew		hews	hewed	hewing			
mew		mews	mewed	mewing		mewer	
pew		pews					
phew	ph						
skew	sk	skews	skewed	skewing		skewer	
spew	sp	spews	spewed	spewing			
view		views	viewed	viewing		viewer	
yew		yews					

** In some dialects, the **EW** in **chew** says /oo/.

Multi-syllable

Base	LT's	-s/-es	-ed	-ing	-y/-ly	-er	-est
curfew	ur	curfews					
nephew	ph	nephews					
pewter	-er						

Exception

Base	LT's	-s/-es	-ed	-ing	-y/-ly	-er	-est
sew		sews	sewed	sewing		sewer	

OU

/ow/ in couch

Position: Middle

Vocalization: Voiced

Classification: Diphthong

Group: Vowel Team, U/W Alternate

Multiple spellings (common) /ow/: OU, OW

Multiple sounds for OU: /ow/ in couch, /oo/ in soup, /ŭ/ in touch, /ō/ in soul.

- The **/ow/** sound is spelled two ways, **OU** and **OW**.
- **W** and **U** often work together as "alternates." **W** combinations (like **OW**) are used at the end of root words, whereas **U** combinations (like **OU**) are used in the middle or beginning of root words. However, **OW** is sometimes used in the middle of a root word, if it is followed by the letters **L** or **N** (**owl**, **town**)
- **OU** that says **/ow/** is a diphthong. A diphthong has two vowel sounds that glide from one sound to another. It is different from a digraph, in that a digraph has two vowels that make one new sound, whereas a diphthong still has two distinct sounds.

Sound	U - Beginning or Middle		W -End	
/aw/	**AU**	cause	**AW**	saw
/yoo/	**EU**	feud	**EW**	few
/oo/			**EW**	blew
/ow/	**OU**	couch	**OW**	cow
/ō/	**OU**	soul	**OW**	snow
/oo/	**OU**	soup		
/ŭ/	**OU**	touch		

OU

couch

- See **OUR** in **R**-combinations in Volume 3 for **OUR** words. **OUR** is listed separately, because it can be easily confused with R-controlled letter teams (**OUR, OR, UR**).

Base	LT's	-s/-es	-ed	-ing	-y/-ly	-er	-est
bounce	-ce	bounces	bounced	bouncing	bouncy	*bouncier*	*bounciest*
bout		bouts					
Chou	ch	Chou's					
cloud	cl	clouds	clouded	clouding	cloudy	*cloudier*	*cloudiest*
couch	ch	couches	couched	couching			
count	nt	counts	counted	counting		counter	
doubt	b*	doubts	doubted	doubting		doubter	
flounce	fl -ce	flounces	flounced	flouncing	flouncy	*flouncier*	*flounciest*
foul		fouls	fouled	fouling			
found	nd						
fount	nt	founts					
gouge	-ge	gouges	gouged	gouging			
gout							
grouch	gr ch	grouches	grouched	grouching	grouchy	*grouchier*	*grouchiest*
ground	gr nd	grounds	grounded	grounding			
grouse	gr -se	grouses	groused	grousing			
grout	gr	grouts	grouted	grouting			
hound	nd	hounds	hounded	hounding			
house	-se	houses	housed	housing			
joust	st	jousts	jousted	jousting			
loud					loudly	louder	loudest
louse	-se	louses					
lout		louts					
mound	nd	mounds	mounded	mounding			
mount	nt	mounts	mounted	mounting			

Base	LT's	-s/-es	-ed	-ing	-y/-ly	-er	-est
mouse	-se				mousy	*mousier*	*mousiest*
noun		nouns					
ouch	ch	ouches					
ounce	-ce	ounces					
out		outs	outed	outing			
pouch	ch	pouches	pouched	pouching			
pounce	-ce	pounces	pounced	pouncing			
pound	nd	pounds	pounded	pounding		pounder	
pout		pouts	pouted	pouting	pouty	*poutier*	*poutiest*
proud	pr				proudly	prouder	proudest
round	nd	rounds	rounded	rounding		rounder	roundest
roust	st	rousts	rousted	rousting			
rout		routs	routed	routing		router	
scout	sc	scouts	scouted	scouting			
Scout	sc	Scout's					
shout	sh	shouts	shouted	shouting		shouter	
shroud	shr	shrouds	shrouded	shrouding			
slouch	sl ch	slouches	slouched	slouching	slouchy	*slouchier*	*slouchiest*
snout	sn	snouts					
sound	nd	sounds	sounded	sounding		Sounder	
south	th						
spouse	sp -se	spouses					
spout	sp	spouts	spouted	spouting			
sprout	spr	sprouts	sprouted	sprouting			
stout	st				stoutly	stouter	stoutest
thou	th						
tout		touts	touted	touting			
trout	tr						
vouch	ch	vouches	vouched	vouching		voucher	

See next page for compound words. **OU**

Compound

Base	LT's	-s/-es	-ed	-ing	-y/-ly	-er	-est
blowout	bl ow	blowouts					
burnout	ur						
buyout	uy	buyouts					
checkout	ch ck	checkouts					
cookout	oo	cookouts					
cutout		cutouts					
dropout	dr	dropouts					
dugout		dugouts					
fallout	all						
handout	nd	handouts					
hangout	ang	hangouts					
hideout	i-e	hideouts					
knockout	kn ck	knockouts					
lockout	ck	lockouts					
lookout	oo	lookouts					
madhouse	-se	madhouses					
outback	ck						
outboard	oar						
outbound	nd						
outbreak	br ea	outbreaks					
outburst	ur st	outbursts					
outcast	st	outcasts					
outclass	cl ss	outclasses					
outcrop	cr	outcrops					
outcry	cr y	outcries					
outdid							
outdoor	oor	outdoors					
outfall	all						
outfield	ie ld	outfields					
outflank	fl ank	outflanks					
outflow	fl ow	outflows					
outfox		outfoxes	outfoxed	outfoxing			
outgoing	ing						
outgrew	gr ew						
outguess	ss gu	outguesses	outguessed	outguessing			
outgun		outguns	outgunned	outgunning			
outhouse	-se	outhouses					
outlast	st	outlasts					

OU

couch

Base	LT's	-s/-es	-ed	-ing	-y/-ly	-er	-est
outlaw	aw	outlaws					

outlet		outlets	
outline	i-e	outlines	
outlive	-ve	outlives	
outlook	oo		
outpace	ace	outpaces	outpaced	outpacing
outplay	pl ay	outplays	outplayed	outplaying
outpost	ost	outposts	
output	u		
outran			
outrank	ank	outranks	outranked	outranking
outright	ight		
outsell	ll	outsells		outselling
outshine	sh i-e	outshines		outshining
outshone	sh o-e		
outside	i-e		
outsize	i-e	outsizes	
outsold	old		
outstrip	str	outstrips	outstripped	outstripping
outtake	a-e	outtakes	
outvote	o-e	outvotes	outvoted	outvoting
outwit		outwits	outwitted	outwitting
outwork	wor	outworks	outworked	outworking
payout	ay	payouts	
shutout	sh	shutouts	
tryout	tr y	tryouts	
turnout	ur	turnouts	
washout	wa sh	washouts	
whiteout	wh i-e	whiteouts	
without	th		
workout	wor	workouts	

<u>OU</u>

/oo/ in soup

Position: Middle

Vocalization: Voiced

Classification: Vowel Digraph

Group: Vowel Team, U/W Alternate

Multiple spellings (common) /ū/ /oo/: U, OO, U-E, EW

Multiple spellings (rare) /ū/ /oo/: UE, <u>OU</u>, EU, UI

Multiple sounds for OU: /ow/ in couch, <u>/oo/ in soup</u>, /ŭ/ in touch, /ō/ in soul.

- **OU** in **out** (previous list) is a diphthong, because you hear two sounds. However, **OU** in **you** (this list) is considered a vowel digraph, because you hear only one sound.
- See **R**-combinations in Volume 3 for **OUR** words.
- **W** and **U** often work together as "alternates." **W** combinations (like **OW**) are used at the end of root words, whereas **U** combinations (like **OU**) are used in the middle or beginning of root words.   Unlike other **U/W** alternates, there is no equivalent ending **OW**-team that matches the **long /oo/** in **soup** (see chart below).
- The word **you** is not a good key word for the **OU /oo/** sound, because the **Y** makes it sound like it is saying **/yoo/.**

See next page for word lists.

198

OU

soup

Sound	U - Beginning or Middle		W -End	
/aw/	AU	cause	AW	saw
/yoo/	EU	feud	EW	few
/oo/			EW	blew
/ow/	OU	couch	OW	cow
/ō/	OU	soul	OW	snow
/oo/	OU	soup		
/ŭ/	OU	touch		

Base	LT's	-s/-es	-ed	-ing	-y/-ly	-er	-est
coup	p*	coups					
ghoul	gh	ghouls					
group	gr	groups	grouped	grouping		grouper	
joule	e*	joules					
mousse	e*						
pouf		poufs					
rouge	-ge						
route	e*	routes	routed	routing		router	
roux	x*						
soup		soups			soupy	*soupier*	*soupiest*
troupe	tr e*	troupes					
wound	nd	wounds	wounded	wounding			
you							
youth	th	youths					

Compound

Base	LT's	-s/-es	-ed	-ing	-y/-ly	-er	-est
newsgroup	ew gr -s	newsgroups					
soupbowl	ow	soupbowls					
playgroup	pl ay gr	playgroups					

OU

/ŭ/ in touch

Position: Middle

Vocalization: Voiced

Classification: Vowel Digraph

Group: Vowel Team, U/W Alternate

Multiple spellings (common) /ŭ/: U, A-, O

Multiple spellings (rare) /ŭ/: OU

Multiple sounds for OU: /ow/ in couch, /oo/ in soup, /ŭ/ in touch, /ō/ in soul.

- **W** and **U** often work together as "alternates." **W** combinations (like **OW**) are used at the end of root words, whereas **U** combinations (like **OU**) are used in the middle or beginning of root words. Unlike other **U/W** alternates, there is no equivalent **OW** sound that matches the /ŭ/ in **touch** (see chart below).

Sound	U - Beginning or Middle		W -End	
/aw/	**AU**	cause	**AW**	saw
/yoo/	**EU**	feud	**EW**	few
/oo/			**EW**	blew
/ow/	**OU**	couch	**OW**	cow
/ō/	**OU**	soul	**OW**	snow
/oo/	**OU**	soup		
/ŭ/	**OU**	touch		

OU

touch

Base	LT's	-s/-es	-ed	-ing	-y/-ly	-er	-est
touch	ch	touches	touched	touching	touchy	*touchier*	*touchiest*
young	ung					younger	youngest

Multi-syllable

Base	LT's	-s/-es	-ed	-ing	-y/-ly	-er	-est
country	-y tr	countries					
couple	ple	couples	coupled	coupling			
cousin		cousins					
double	ble	doubles	doubled	doubling	doubly		
couplet	pl	couplets					

OU that says /ŭ/ is a part of the suffix -OUS

Base	LT's	-s/-es	-ed	-ing	-y/-ly	-er	-est
anxious	i*				anxiously		
arduous	ar				arduously		
aqueous	qu						
bulbous							
callous *	all*				callously		
copious	i*				copiously		
curious *	ur* i*				curiously		
devious	i*				deviously		
furious	i*				furiously		
hideous					hideously		
igneous							

OU

/ō/ in soul

Position: Middle

Vocalization: Voiced

Classification: Vowel Digraph

Group: Vowel Team, U/W Alternate

Multiple spellings (common) /ō/: O, O-E, OA, OW

Multiple spellings (rare) /ō/: OE, OU

Multiple sounds for OU: /ow/ in couch, /oo/ in soup, /ŭ/ in touch, /ō/ in soul.

- The **OU** in soul is found primarily in words with longer letter teams, such as **OUR** and **OUGH**. See Volume 3 for those letter teams.
- **W** and **U** often work together as "alternates." **W** combinations (like **OW**) are used at the end of root words **(snow)**, whereas **U** combinations (like **OU**) are used in the middle or beginning of root words **(soul)**.

Sound	U - Beginning or Middle		W -End	
/aw/	**AU**	cause	**AW**	saw
/yoo/	**EU**	feud	**EW**	few
/oo/			**EW**	blew
/ow/	**OU**	couch	**OW**	cow
/ō/	**OU**	soul	**OW**	snow
/oo/	**OU**	soup		
/ŭ/	**OU**	touch		

202

OU

soul

Base	LT's	-s/-es	-ed	-ing	-y/-ly	-er	-est
soul		souls					

Compound

Base	LT's	-s/-es	-ed	-ing	-y/-ly	-er	-est
boulder	er	boulders					
cantaloupe	e*	cantaloupes					
poultice	-ce	poultices					
poultry	tr -y						
shoulder	sh ld er	shoulders	shouldered	shouldering			
soulless	ss				soullessly		

OW

/ow/ in cow

Position: End, Middle (in front of L or N)

Vocalization: Voiced

Classification: Diphthong

Group: Vowel Team, U/W Alternate

Multiple spellings (common) /ow/: OU, OW

Multiple sounds for OW: /ow/ in cow, /ō/ in snow

- **W** and **U** often work together as "alternates." **W** combinations (like **OW**) are used at the end of root words **(cow)**, whereas **U** combinations (like **OU**) are used in the middle or beginning of root words **(couch)**. (See exception below).
- Although **OW /ow/** in **cow** is usually found at the end of a word, it can also be found in the middle of a root word if it is followed by the letters **L** or **N (owl, gown)**. The /ō/ in **snow** (the alternate sound) can also be followed by the letters **L** or **N (bowl, own)**, so the letters **L** and **N** cannot be used to determine the sound of the **OW**.
- When **OW** says **/ow/** in **cow**, **OW** is a diphthong. A diphthong has two vowel sounds that glide from one sound to another. It is different from a digraph, in that a digraph has two vowels that make one new sound, whereas a diphthong has two distinct sounds.

See next page for word lists.

204

OW

cow

Sound	U - Beginning or Middle		W -End	
/aw/	AU	cause	AW	saw
/yoo/	EU	feud	EW	few
/oo/			EW	blew
/ow/	OU	couch	OW	cow
/ō/	OU	soul	OW	snow
/oo/	OU	soup		
/ŭ/	OU	touch		

Base	LT's	-s/-es	-ed	-ing	-y/-ly	-er	-est
bow		bows	bowed	bowing		bower	
brow	br	brows					
brown	br	browns	browned	browning		browner	brownest
chow	ch	chows	chowed	chowing			
clown	cl	clowns	clowned	clowning			
cow		cows	cowed	cowing		cower	
crowd	cr	crowds	crowded	crowding			
crown	cr	crowns	crowned	crowning			
down		downs	downed	downing	downy	downer	
frown	fr	frowns	frowned	frowning	frowny		
gown		gowns					
growl	gr	growls	growled	growling	growly	growler	
how							
howl		howls	howled	howling		howler	
jowl		jowls					
now							
owl		owls					
plow	pl	plows	plowed	plowing			
pow						power	
prow	pr	prows					
prowl	pr	prowls	prowled	prowling		prowler	
scowl	sc	scowls	scowled	scowling		scowler	
town		towns					
vow		vows	vowed	vowing			
wow		wows	wowed	wowing			
yowl		yowls	yowled	yowling		yowler	

OW

Compound

Base	LT's	-s/-es	-ed	-ing	-y/-ly	-er	-est
anyhow	-y						
breakdown	br ea						
browbeat	br ea	browbeats					
brownfield	br ie ld	brownfields					
countdown	ou nt	countdowns					
cowbell	ll	cowbells					
cowboy	oy	cowboys					
cowgirl	ir	cowgirls					

Compound

Base	LT's	-s/-es	-ed	-ing	-y/-ly	-er	-est
cowhand	nd	cowhands					
cowpat		cowpats					
crosstown	cr ss						
downbeat	ea	downbeats					
downcast	st						
downfall	all	downfalls					
downgrade	gr a-e	downgrades	downgraded	downgrading			
download	oa	downloads	downloaded	downloading			
downplay	pl ay	downplays	downplayed	downplaying			
downpour	our	downpours					
downright	ight						
downriver	-er						
downscale	sc a-e	downscales					
downshift	sh ft	downshifts					
downside	i-e						
downsize	i-e	downsizes	downsized	downsizing			
downstage	st age						
downswing	sw ing	downswings					
downtown		downtowns					
downtrend	tr nd	downtrends					
downturn	ur	downturns					
downward	war						
downwind	nd						
eyebrow	br e-e*	eyebrows					
highbrow	igh br						
hoedown	oe	hoedowns					

OW

cow

Base	LT's	-s/-es	-ed	-ing	-y/-ly	-er	-est
knockdown	kn ck	knockdowns					
letdown		letdowns					
markdown	ar	markdowns					
meltdown	lt	meltdowns					
nightgown	ight	nightgowns					
overcrowd	er cr	overcrowds	overcrowded	overcrowding			
rundown							
shutdown	sh	shutdowns					
snowplow**	sn pl	snowplows					
sundown							
touchdown	ou ch	touchdowns					
townhouse	ou -se	townhouses					

****Snowplow** has both sounds for **OW** in one word.

OW

/ō/ in snow

Position: End, Middle (in front of L or N)

Vocalization: Voiced

Classification: Vowel Digraph

Group: Vowel Team, U/W Alternate

Multiple spellings (common) /ō/: O, O-E, OA, <u>OW</u>

Multiple spellings (rare) /ō/: OE, OU

Multiple sounds for OW: /ow/ in cow, <u>/ō/ in snow</u>

- **W** and **U** often work together as "alternates." **W** combinations (like **OW**) are used at the end of root words **(cow)**, whereas **U** combinations (like **OU**) are used in the middle or beginning of root words **(couch).** (See exception below).

- Although **OW** /ō/ in **snow** is usually found at the end of a word, it can also be found in the middle of a root word if it is followed by the letters **L** or **N (bowl, own)**. **OW** /ow/ in **cow** (the alternate sound) can also be followed by the letters **L** or **N (owl, gown)**, so the letters **L** and **N** cannot be used to determine the sound of the **OW**. Students will need to use context to determine the sound of **OW** in these words.

- Although **OW** in **cow** is diphthong, **OW** in **snow** is a digraph because the **O** and **W** make one sound together.

OW

snow

Sound	U - Beginning or Middle		W -End	
/aw/	**AU**	cause	**AW**	saw
/yoo/	**EU**	feud	**EW**	few
/oo/			**EW**	blew
/ow/	**OU**	couch	**OW**	cow
/ō/	**OU**	soul	**OW**	snow
/oo/	**OU**	soup		
/ŭ/	**OU**	touch		

Base	LT's	-s/-es	-ed	-ing	-y/-ly	-er	-est
blow	bl	blows		blowing	blowy	blower	
blown	bl						
bowl		bowls	bowled	bowling		bowler	
crow	cr	crows	crowed	crowing			
Crow	cr						
flow	fl	flows	flowed	flowing	flowy		
flown	fl						
glow	gl	glows	glowed	glowing			
grow	gr	grows		growing		grower	
grown	gr						
know	kn	knows		knowing		knower	
known	kn						
low		lows	lowed	lowing	lowly	lower	lowest
mow		mows	mowed	mowing		mower	
mown							
own		owns	owned	owning		owner	
row		rows	rowed	rowing		rower	
show	sh	shows	showed	showing	showy	*showier*	*showiest*
shown	sh						
slow	sl	slows	slowed	slowing		slower	slowest
snow	sn	snows	snowed	snowing	snowy	snowier	*snowiest*
sown							
stow	st	stows	stowed	stowing			
throw	thr	throws		throwing		thrower	
thrown	thr						
tow		tows	towed	towing			

209

OW

snow

Compound

Base	LT's	-s/-es	-ed	-ing	-y/-ly	-er	-est
airflow	air fl						
blowhole	bl o-e	blowholes					
blowout	bl ou	blowouts					
crowbar	cr ar	crowbars					
fishbowl	sh	fishbowls					
hedgerow	dge	hedgerows					
ingrown	gr						
longbow	ong	longbows					
lowdown**	ow						
outflow	ou fl	outflows					
outgrowth	ou gr th	outgrowths					
overblown	er bl						
overflown	er fl						
overgrown	er gr						
overthrow	er thr	overflows	overflowed	overflowing			
rainbow	ai	rainbows					
roadshow	oa sh	roadshows					
rowboat	oa	rowboats					
scarecrow	sc are cr	scarecrows					
showcase	sh a-e	showcases	showcased	showcasing			
showdown**	sh ow	showdowns					
showgirl	sh ir	showgirls					
showoff	sh ff	showoffs					
showplace	sh pl ace	showplaces					
showroom	sh oo	showrooms					
showtime	sh i-e	showtimes					
sideshow	i-e sh	sideshows					
slowdown**	ow sl	slowdowns					
slowpoke	sl o-e	slowpokes					
snowball	sn all	snowballs					
snowboard	sn oar	snowboards					
snowbound	sn ou nd						
snowdrift	sn dr ft	snowdrifts					
snowfall	sn all	snowfalls					
snowman	sn						
snowplow**	sn pl	snowplows					

** The words **lowdown**, **showdown**, **slowdown**, and **snowplow** all have both the /ow/ and /ō/ sounds.

210

snow

Compound

Base	LT's	-s/-es	-ed	-ing	-y/-ly	-er	-est
snowshoe	sn sh oe	snowshoes					
snowsuit	sn ui	snowsuits					
throwaway	thr a- ay						
throwback	thr ck	throwbacks					
towpath	th	towpaths					
towrope	o-e	towropes					
undertow	er						
washbowl	wa sh	washbowls					

*lowdown, slowdown, and snowplow all have both sounds for OW.

Sounds of Y
Printable Cards

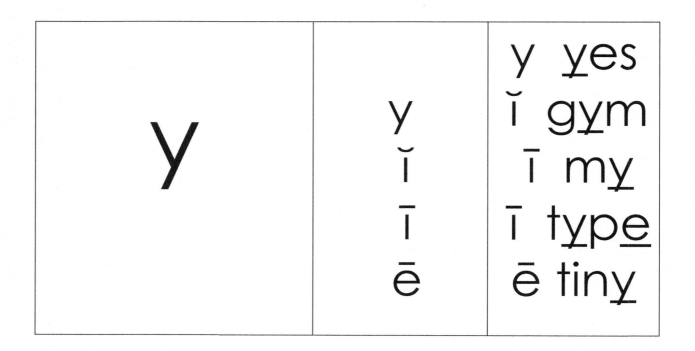

See Resources section for Sounds of Y charts.

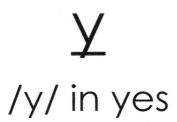

/y/ in yes

Position: Beginning

Vocalization: Voiced

Classification: Consonant

Group: Y sounds

Multiple spellings /y/: <u>Only Y</u>

Multiple sounds for Y: See below

- **Y** in **yes** is the only instance where **Y** is a consonant. In all other cases, **Y** is a vowel.

Sounds of Y

Y at the **beginning** of a root word says /y/ in **yam**.
Y in the **middle** of a root word says / ĭ/ in **gym**.
Y at the **end** of a root word says / ī / in **my**.
Y as a part of the **VCE** pattern **Y-E** says says / ī / in **type**.
Y at the end of a multi-syllable word) says /ē/ in **tiny**.
Y-suffixes: **-Y** in **fishy**, **-LY** in **deeply**, **-EY** in **donkey**

See next page for word list.

y

yes

Base	LT's	-s/-es	-ed	-ing	-y/-ly	-er	-est
yack	ck	yacks	yacked	yacking			
yak		yaks					
yam		yams					
yank	ank	yanks	yanked	yanking			
yap		yaps	yapped	yapping	yappy	yapper	
yard	ar	yards					
yarn	ar	yarns					
yawn	aw	yawns	yawned	yawning		yawner	
yeah	ea h						
year	ear	years			yearly		
yell	ll	yells	yelled	yelling		yeller	
yelp	lp	yelps	yelped	yelping		yelper	
yen							
yes		yeses					
yet							
yin							
yip		yips	yipped	yipping	yippy		
yolk	olk	yolks					
yon							
you	ou						
your	our						
yowl	ow	yowls	yowled	yowling		yowler	
yuck	ck				yucky	*yuckier*	*yuckiest*
yum					yummy	*yummier*	*yummiest*

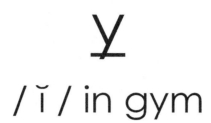

/ ĭ / in gym

Position: Middle

Vocalization: Voiced

Classification: Y as a Vowel

Group: Y sounds

Multiple spellings (common) / ĭ /: I, <u>Y</u>

Multiple spellings (rare) / ĭ /: UI

Multiple sounds for Y: See below

- **Y** in **gym** is one of the only times the letter **Y** appears in the middle of a root word.
- Both Greek and Latin used **Y** as a short **/ ĭ /** sound.
- The letter **Y** in the middle of a root word is very rare. Usually in alternates, the **I** letter team **(OI, UI)** is found in the middle of a word, and the **Y** letter team **(OY, UY)** is found at the end of a word.

<u>Sounds of Y</u>

Y at the **beginning** of a root word says **/y/** in **yam**.
Y in the **middle** of a root word says **/ ĭ/** in **gym**.
Y at the **end** of a root word says **/ ī /** in **my**.
Y as a part of the **VCE** pattern **Y-E** says says **/ ī /** in **type**.
Y at the **end** of a multi-syllable word) says **/ē/** in **tiny**.
Y-suffixes: **-Y** in **fishy**, **-LY** in **deeply** , **-EY** in **donkey**

---

y

gym

Base	LT's	-s/-es	-ed	-ing	-y/-ly	-er	-est
crypt	cr pt	crypts					
cyst	st	cysts					
gym		gyms					
gyp		gyps	gypped	gypping			
hymn	mn	hymns					
lymph	ph						
myrrh	rh						
myth	th	myths					
onyx	y						

y

my

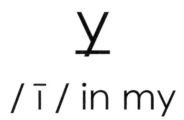

/ī/ in my

Position: End

Vocalization: Voiced

Classification: Vowel

Group: Y sounds, Open syllable

Multiple spellings (common) /ī/: I, I-E, Y, IGH

Multiple spellings (rare) /ī/: Y-E, IE, -YE, UY

Multiple sounds for Y: See below

- The **Y** in **my** is an open syllable, similar to **O** in **go** and **E** in **me**.

Sounds of Y

Y at the **beginning** of a root word says **/y/** in **yam**.
Y in the **middle** of a root word says **/ĭ/** in **gym**.
Y at the **end** of a root word says **/ī/** in **my**.
Y as a part of the **VCE** pattern **Y-E** says says **/ī/** in **type**.
Y at the end of a multi-syllable word) says **/ē/** in **tiny**.
Y-suffixes: **-Y** in **fishy**, **-LY** in **deeply**, **-EY** in **donkey**

See next page for word lists.

217

Base	LT's	-s/-es	-ed	-ing	-y/-ly	-er	-est
by							
cry	cr	cries	cried	crying		crier	
dry	dr	dries	dried	drying	dryly	dryer/drier	driest
fly	fl	flies	flied	flying		flyer	
fry	fr	fries	fried	frying		fryer	
my							
ply	pl	plies	plied	plying		pliers	
pry	pr	pries	pried	prying			
shy	sh	shies	shied	shying	shyly	shyer	shyest
sky	sk	skies					
sly	sl				slyly	slyer	slyest
spry	spr				spryly		
spy	sp	spies	spied	spying			
sty	st	sties					
thy	th						
try	tr	tries	tried	trying			
why	wh						
wry	wr				wryly	wryer	wryest

y

/ē/ in tiny

Position: End

Vocalization: Voiced

Classification: Vowel

Group: Y sounds

Multiple spellings (common) /ē/: E, -Y, EA, EE, -EY, E-E

Multiple spellings (rare) /ē/: IE, EI, -AE

Multiple sounds for Y: See chart below

- One syllable words with **Y** at the end say long **I** (fly). Two or more syllable words with a **Y** at the end say long **/ē/.** The suffix **-Y** at the end of a word also says long**/ē/.** Any time you add the suffix **-Y** to a one syllable root word, it becomes a multi-syllable word.
- This list could possibly have been combined with the **-Y** suffix list. Most **-Y** endings of multisyllable words are suffixes, and even the words in this list that don't obviously have a base word may have had a root that had a **-Y** added to it. Some are more obviously suffixes, and some were suffixed back in history. The good news is that most multi-syllable words end in **Y** saying long **/ē/,** so students do not need to differentiate.
- Many of the two-syllable **-Y** words have a long first vowel. The reason why is not clear, but some of these root words may have had a silent **E** originally that was dropped when the **– Y** was added. For example, the word **tiny** comes from the word **tine** or **tyne**, and when the **-Y** was added, the **E** was dropped (etymonline.com). This also explains why the **AR** in these words says **/air/,** and not **/ar/.** The word **wary** comes from the word **ware**, "to take heed of, beware." When the **-Y** was added, the **E** in ware was dropped. (etymology information from etymonline.com)

219

y

tiny

- Syllable division - The short vowel words will be divided after the closing consonant **(cop-y, lev-y)**. The long vowel words will be divided after the vowel **(ba-by, du-ty)**.

Sounds of Y

Y at the **beginning** of a root word says /y/ in **yam**.
Y in the **middle** of a root word says / ĭ/ in **gym**.
Y at the **end** of a root word says / ī / in **my**.
Y as a part of the **VCE** pattern **Y-E** says says / ī / in **type**.
Y at the end of a multi-syllable word) says /ē/ in **tiny**.
Y-suffixes: **-Y** in **fishy**, **-LY** in **deeply** , **-EY** in **donkey**

Two syllable -Y words

Base	LT's	-s/-es	-ed	-ing	-y/-ly	-er	-est
baby							
bevy							
body		bodies					
busy		busies	busied	busying			
city	c(i)	cities					
Cody		Cody's					
copy		copies	copied	copying		copier	
cozy		cozies	cozied	cozying		cozier	coziest
duly							
duty		duties					
envy		envies	envied	envying		envier	
fury	ur(e)	furies					
Gary	ar(e)	Gary's					
holy		holies				holier	holiest
Jody		Jody's					

y

tiny

Base	LT's	-s/-es/'s	-ed	-ing	-y/-ly	-er	-est
jury	ur(e)	juries	juried				
lady		ladies					
levy		levies	levied	levying			
lily							
Lily		Lily's					
many							
Mary		Mary's					
navy							
Navy		Navy's					
pity		pities	pitied	pitying			
pony		ponies	ponied	ponying			
posy		posies					
puny							
Ruby		Ruby's					
tidy		tidies	tidied	tidying			
tiny						tinier	tiniest
Toby		Toby's					
Tony		Tony's					
vary	ar(e)	varies	varied	varying			
very	er*						
wary	ar(e)					warier	wariest
zany						zanier	zaniest

-y

/ē/ in fishy

Position: End

Vocalization: Voiced

Classification: Suffix

Group: Y sounds, Suffix

Multiple spellings (common) /ē/: E, -Y, EA, EE, -EY, E-E

Multiple spellings (rare) /ē/: IE, EI, -AE

Multiple sounds for Y: See box below

- See the lists in this book for **-EY (Y/E Alternates)** and **-LY** words. For words with **-CY** (soft **C**), and **-GY** (soft **G**), see volume 3.
- All of the lists in this book have a **-Y** column. The list below is only a sample. For more words, consult the **-Y** column in each list, or see Volume 3, simple suffixes for more extensive lists.
- One syllable words with **Y** at the end say long **/ ī / (fly)**. Two or more syllable words with a **Y** at the end say long **/ē/**. The suffix **-Y** at the end of a word also says long**/ē/**. Any time you add the suffix **-Y** to a word, that word becomes a multi-syllable word.
- To make a plural, words that end in **-Y** change the **Y** to **I**, and add **-ES** (**piggy, piggies**). However, words that end in the letter **Y**, where the **Y** is a part of a vowel team (**OY, EY**), do not follow this rule and only add **-S** (**boys, plays**). See **AY** for **AY** exceptions to this rule.
- When adding a vowel suffix to a word that ends in **Y**, the **Y** does not change to **I** if the vowel suffix being added starts with an **I**, because that would cause a double **I** in the word. Words of English origin do not double the letter **I**. For **party – partying** there is no change in the **Y** because the suffix **-ING** begins with an **I**. For **party – parties**, the **Y** changes to **I**, because the suffix **-ES** starts with an **E** and not an **I**.

Sounds of Y

Y at the **beginning** of a root word says /y/ in **yam**.
Y in the **middle** of a root word says / ĭ/ in **gym**.
Y at the **end** of a root word says / ī / in **my**.
Y as a part of the **VCE** pattern **Y-E** says says / ī / in **type**.
Y at the end of a multi-syllable word) says /ē/ in **tiny**.
Y-suffixes: **-Y** in **fishy**, **-LY** in **deeply** , **-EY** in **donkey**

Adding Y as a suffix:

- The **1-1-1- Rule** – When you add a vowel suffix (such as **-Y**) to a base word, you double the ending consonant if the following applies to the word:
  It has 1 syllable, it has 1 short vowel, and it ends in 1 consonant. **(pig – piggy)**
- When a word ends in an **E**, you drop the **E** before adding a vowel suffix (like **Y**)
  shine – shiny

1-1-1 Rule	No doubling (not 1-1-1)	Silent E Words (drop E rule)
Dad Daddy	chew chewy	shake shaky
gas gassy	bush bushy	shade shady
Peg Peggy	fish fishy	shine shiny
pen penny	mush mushy	ease easy
pep peppy	push pushy	edge edgy
pig piggy	slush slushy	haze hazy
wit witty	squish squishy	nose nosy
dog doggy	length lengthy	ware wary
fog foggy	thorn thorny	brine briny
bud buddy	thirst thirsty	
bug buggy	thin thinly	
cub cubby	show showy	
fun funny	grain grainy	
gum gummy	hair hairy	
chat chatty	bead beady	
chill chilly	leaf leafy	
chum chummy	peach peachy	
bag baggy	cheese cheesy	
bug buggy	greed greedy	

-ly

/ē/ in curly

Position: End

Vocalization: Voiced

Classification: Suffix

Group: Y sounds, Suffix

Multiple spellings (common) /lē/: Only -LY

Multiple sounds for LY: Only /lee/

- The list below is only a sample. All of the lists in this book have an **-LY** column.

Sounds of Y

Y at the **beginning** of a root word says /y/ in **yam**.
Y in the **middle** of a root word says / ĭ/ in **gym**.
Y at the **end** of a root word says / ī / in **my**.
Y as a part of the **VCE** pattern **Y-E** says says / ī / in **type**.
Y at the end of a multi-syllable word) says /ē/ in **tiny**.
Y-suffixes: **-Y** in **fishy**, **-LY** in **deeply** , **-EY** in **donkey**

See next page for **-LY** list

-LY suffix		
amply mp	hardly ar	pebbly
badly	hotly	poorly oor
barely are	hugely uge	rally
boldly old	justly st	rarely are
bubbly	kindly ind	rashly sh
calmly alm	lately a-e	really ea
coldly old	likely i-e	richly ch
costly ost	lively i-e	rudely u-e
coyly oy	lonely o-e	sadly
cuddly	loudly ou	safely a-e
curly ur	*lovely o-e**	scaly sc a-e
curtly ur	lowly ow	seemly ee
daily ai	madly	shyly sh y
damply mp	mainly ai	simply mp
dearly ear	manly	slowly sl ow
deeply ee	meanly ea	softly ft
diddly	measly ea	steely st ee
dimly	meekly ee	surly ur
early ear	merely ere	thinly th
evenly e-e	mildly ild	timely i-e
fairly air	mostly ost	vastly st
feebly ee	nearly ear	warmly war
firmly ir	neatly ea	weakly ea
flatly fl	newly ew	wetly
fondly nd	nicely ice	wildly ild
gently nt	oddly	yearly ear
gladly gl	pearly ear	
godly		

Resources

Auditory Drill Paper - Example

b	c	d	f	g	h	j
k	l	m	n	p	q	r
s	t	v	w	x	y	z
a	ay	a-e	e	ee	e-e	i
y	i-e	y-e	o	o-e	ow	u
u-e	th	ch	sh			

Auditory Drill Paper

Compound Word Frame - Example

stair	case

base	board

suit	case

book	case

milk	shake

hand	shake

take	off

Compound Word Frame

Go Fish Playing Cards - Example

th	th	sh	sh
ch	ch	wh	wh
ph	ph	rh	rh

Fish Illustration source - Pixabay,Image-3736

Go Fish Playing Cards

Blank Playing Cards - Example

sh	sh	th	th
ch	ch	wh	wh
ph	ph	rh	rh

Blank Playing Cards

Phoneme Spelling

b	ea	ch			beach

r	e	m	ote		remote

f	oo	t	b	all	football

l	ea	sh			leash

i	n	s	ide		inside

s	i	st	er		sister

Phoneme Spelling

Phonogram Word Frame (5 elements) – Example

sh	i	p		

t	oo	th		

w	i	th	ou	t

Phonogram Word Frame

Phonogram Word Frame (Wide Spacing) - Example

spr	ing		

squ	i	sh	ing

f	u	dge	

d	oor	w	ay

l	u	nch	

Phonogram Word Frame (Wide Spacing)

Reading and Spelling Word List (narrow lined) – Example

sing _____

bring _____

fling _____

king _____

wing _____

ring _____

Reading and Spelling Word List

_____

_____

_____

_____

_____

_____

_____

_____

_____

_____

VCE Blending Board A,E,I– Example

Use Spelling & Blending Tiles, or write in the spaces.

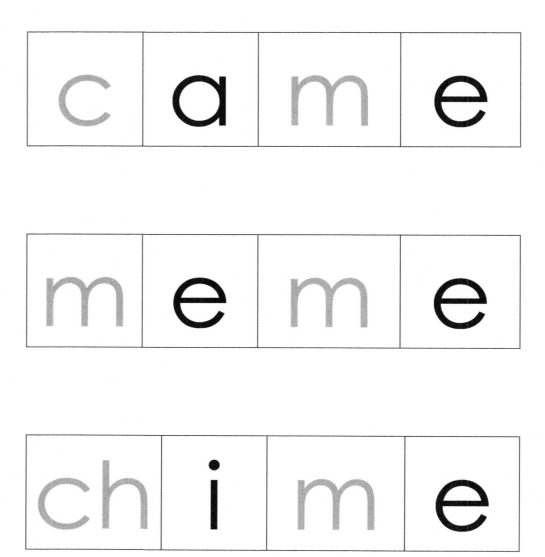

VCE Blending Board – A,E,I

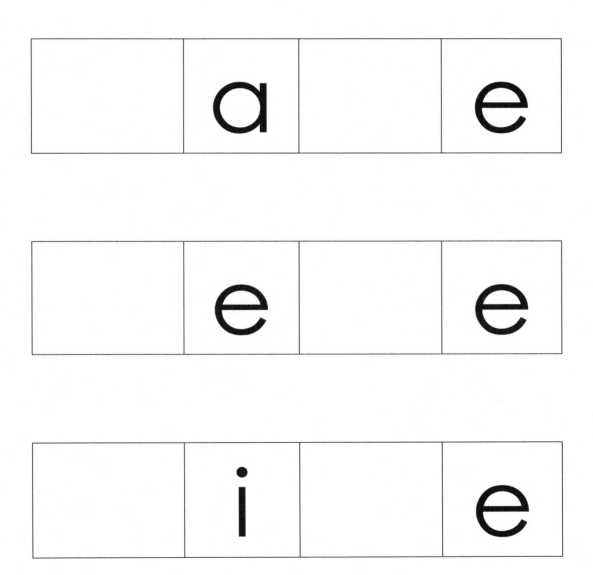

VCE Blending Board – O, U, Y - Example

s h	o	n	e

c	u	t	e

t	y	p	e

VCE Blending Board – O, U, Y

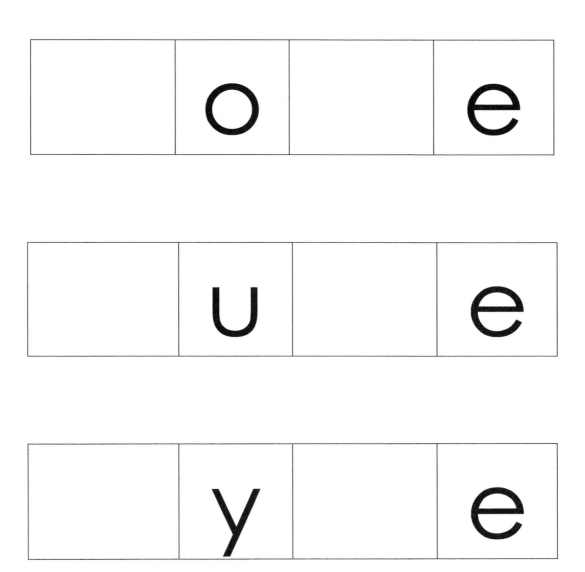

VCE Blending Boards

b	a	k	e
m	e	m	e
t	i	m	e
b	o	n	e
r	u	l	e
t	y	p	e

VCE Blending Boards

	a		e
	e		e
	i		e
	o		e
	u		e
	y		e

Word Segmentation – Example

| thinking | th | ink | ing | | |

| smooth | sm | oo | th | | |

| withdraw | w | i | th | dr | aw |

| wheel | wh | ee | l | | |

| whoosh | wh | oo | sh | | |

| healthy | h | ea | l | th | y |

Word Segmentation

Word Sums (narrow lined) – Example

Word sums help a student practice spelling and how to add on suffixes, or combine more than one word element. Below is an example of a student who is learning to drop -E when -ED is added.

bake + -ed = baked

box + -ed = boxed

poke + -ed = poked

spill + -ed = spilled

_____ + _____ = _____

_____ + _____ = _____

_____ + _____ = _____

_____ + _____ = _____

_____ + _____ = _____

_____ + _____ = _____

_____ + _____ = _____

Word Sums (narrow lined) – Example

_____ + _____ = _____

_____ + _____ = _____

_____ + _____ = _____

_____ + _____ = _____

_____ + _____ = _____

_____ + _____ = _____

_____ + _____ = _____

_____ + _____ = _____

_____ + _____ = _____

_____ + _____ = _____

_____ + _____ = _____

_____ + _____ = _____

Sounds of Y

/y/ in yes
Beginning of words, consonant

/ ĭ / in gym
Words of Greek origin

/ ī / in by
End of one-syllable words, vowel

/ ī / in type
VCE pattern, vowel

/ē/ in tiny
End of multi-syllable words

Y in Digraphs

AY in play

EY in they

OY in toy

Y in Suffixes

-Y in fishy

-EY in honey

-LY in slowly

Positions and Sounds of Y – with cues

Beginning - /y/ in yes

y		

Middle - short /i/ in gym

	y	

End – one syllable - long /i/ in fly

		y

With silent E – Long /i/ in type

	y		e

Suffix - multi-syllable words (tiny) & Suffix Y words – (fishy)

_____y

Positions and Sounds of Y

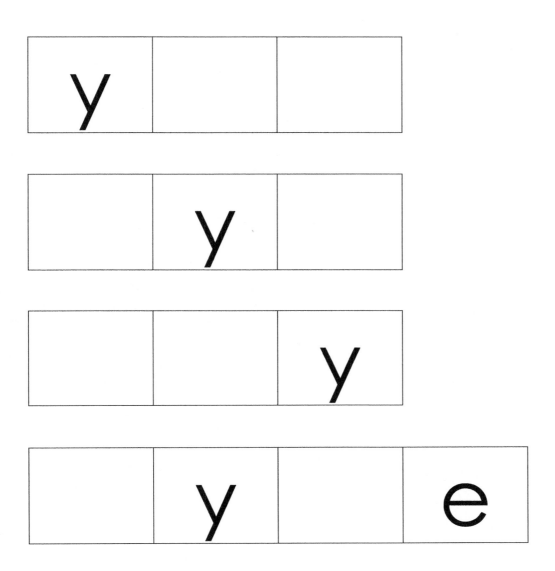

Y Digraph Frame

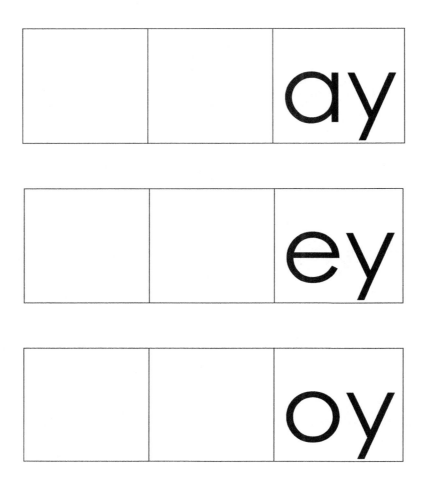

Y Suffix Frame

_____y

_____ly

_____ey

Jobs of the letter E

- **E** is a short vowel in one-syllable words **(bed).**

- **E** is a long vowel in open syllables **(e-rase).**

- **E** can make the preceding vowel long in **VCE** words (**tone**).
  A-E, E-E, I-E, O-E, U-E, Y-E

- **E** is a part of many vowel teams.
  EE, EER, EA, EAR, EY, EI, IE, AE, OE, UE, YE, EW, EU, ER, IER, OAR

- **E** can make the **C** and **G** say their soft sounds (**celery, giraffe**). Teams: **CE, CI, CEI, GE, GI, -CE, -GE, DGE.**

- **E** prevents **U** and **V** from being the last letter in a word (**have, glue**). Teams: **-UE, -VE**

- **E** provides a vowel to the **C-le** syllable pattern (**able, candle**). Teams: **BLE, CLE, CKLE, DLE, FLE, GLE, KLE, PLE, TLE, STLE, ZLE**

- **E** shows that a word ending in the **/s/** sound (for words ending in **S** and **Z**) is not plural (**house, nurse, gauze**). Teams: **-SE, -ZE**

- **E** is sometimes used to distinguish between two words (**on, one**).

- In some words, there is a silent **E** because the **E** sound was originally pronounced out loud, and the spelling has been retained (**come**).

Multiple and Single Spellings - Consonants

Sound	Common Spellings (Over 50 Words)	Uncommon Spellings (Under 50 Words)
/b/	B	
/d/	D, -ED	
/f/	F, PH, FF	GH
/g/	G, GU	GH, GUE
/h/	H	WH
/j/	G, J, -GE, -DGE	
/k/	C, K, CK, CH	QUE
/ks/	X	
/l/	L, LL	
/m/	M	MB, MN
/n/	N	KN, GN, PN
/p/	P	
/qu/	QU	
/r/	R	WR, RH
/s/	S, C, SS, -SE, -CE, SC	PS
/t/	T, -ED	
/v/	V, -VE	
/w/	W, WH	
/y/ yes	Y	
/z/	S, Z, -SE, -ZE	ZZ, X

Multiple and Single Spellings – Blends

Sound	Common Spellings (Over 50 Words)	Uncommon Spellings (Under 50 Words)
/bl/	BL, -BLE	
/br/	BR	
/cl/	CL, -CKLE	-CLE, -KLE
/cr/	CR	
/dl/	-DLE	
/dr/	DR	
/dw/		DW
/fl/	FL	-FLE
/fr/	FR	
/gl/	GL, -GLE	
/gr/	GR	
/pl/	PL	-PLE
/pr/	PR	
/sk/	SC, SK	SCH
/sl/	SL	-STLE
/sm/	SM	
/sn/	SN	
/sp/	SP	
/st/	ST	
/sw/	SW	
/tl/	-TLE	
/tr/	TR	
/tw/	TW	
/zl/		-ZLE
/scr/	SCR	
/spl/	SPL	
/spr/	SPR	
/str/	STR	

Multiple and Single Spellings - Vowels

Short Vowel Sounds

Sound	Common Spellings (Over 50 words)	Uncommon Spellings (under 50 words)
/ă/	A	
/ĕ/	E, EA	
/ĭ/	I, Y	UI
/ŏ/***	O, AW, AU	*
/ŭ/	U, A-**	OU

*Some people list **OUGH** and **AUGH** as a multiple spelling for /ŏ/. I have removed them as spellings for /ŏ/ in this list, because **AUGH** and **OUGH** only say /ŏ/ when they are combined with **T** (OUGHT and AUGHT). It would therefore be more appropriate to teach them as **OUGHT** and **AUGHT**. In addition, **OUGH** has many sounds when it is found without a **T** and /ŏ/ is not one of them. If your curriculum adds **AUGH** and **OUGH** for short /ŏ/, you can add them to the chart.
This chart includes the **A- (**adopt, about**), because it is usually taught as a stand-alone phonogram, but I have not included other schwa sounds. Any vowel can have a schwa sound. Schwa often sounds like short /ŭ/. Sometimes it sounds like the other short vowels, and schwa can also be silent.
***Short /ŏ/ can have very different sounds based on dialect, and even in different words in the same dialect. If you listen to the short /ŏ/ sounds in the word **hot dog**, you can hear two different sounds for **O**. In some areas, the spelling **AW/AU** will make more of a diphthong sound, and will therefore not be included in the multiple spelling of short /ŏ/.

Long Vowel Sounds

Sound	Common Spellings (Over 50 words)	Uncommon Spellings (under 50 words)
/ā/	A, A-E, AI, AY	EI, EY, EA, EIGH, AE
/ē/	E, -Y, EA, EE, -EY, E-E	IE, EI, -AE
/ī/	I, I-E, Y, IGH	Y-E, IE, -YE, UY
/ō/	O, O-E, OA, OW	OE, OU
/ū/ /yoo/	U, U-E, EW	UE, EU
/ū/ /oo/ (moon)	U, OO, U-E, EW	UE, OU, EU, UI

Vowel Sound Teams

Sound	Common Spellings (Over 50 words)	Uncommon Spellings (under 50 words)
short /oo/ (book)	OO	U
/oy/	OI, OY	
/ow/	OU, OW	

Multiple and Single Spellings - Teams

Digraphs & Trigraphs

Sound	Common Spellings (Over 50 words)	Uncommon Spellings (under 50 words)
/ch/	CH, TCH	
/sh/**	SH	CH
/th/ unvoiced	TH	
/th/ voiced	TH	
/chr/	CR	CHR
/sch/	SC, SK	SCH
/shr/		SHR
/squ/		SQU
/thr/		THR

Some people include **SI, TI, and **CI** as sounds of **SH,** due to their auditory position in combinations such as **SION, TIAL,** and **CIAN.**

R-Controlled & R-Combination Sound Teams

Sound	Common Spellings (Over 50 words)	Uncommon Spellings (under 50 words)
/air/*	ARE, AIR, ARR, ERR	EAR
/ar/	AR	
/ear/*	EAR, EER, IRR	ERE, IER
/er/ *	ER, UR, IR, -OR, -AR, URR	EAR, ORR*
/ire/	IRE	YRE
/or/	OR, ORE, OAR	ORR, OOR, OUR
/our/	OUR	

*The spoken sound of **R**-combinations varies widely by dialect. **ORR** especially may sound ore like **ER** or **OR**

*Double **R** spellings (**IRR** in **mirror**, **ARR** in **carry**, **URR** in **burr**) are often formed as part of Chameleon prefixes (**irrevocable = in + revocable**). However, there are still many words that contain these **RR** combinations but are not clearly part of a Chameleon prefix.

Other

/shun/**	TION, SION	CIAN
/zh/**	S, Z, -GE	
/zhun/	SION	

There are currently three differences of opinion on how the suffix **ION / TION should be taught (see below). In my personal opinion, the traditional phonics approach (1) is better for reading instruction, and the morphological approach (2) is useful when explaining the spelling rules, such as when to use **TION, SION** and **CIAN.**

1) From a phonics approach as a whole letter team **(TION)** /shun/. (Traditional Orton-Gillingham)
2) From a morphological approach as the end of a root **(T)**, plus a suffix **(ION)=(T+ION)**
3) From a phonics approach as a combination of letter teams **(TI+ON)** /sh/ + /un/

Multiple and Single Spellings – Teams

Sound	Common Spellings (Over 50 Words)	Uncommon Spellings (Under 50 Words)
/ng/	NG -ang, ing, ong, ung	
/nk/	NK – ank, ink, onk, unk	
/ild/	ILD	
/ind/	IND	
/old/	OLD	
/oll/	OLL	
/ost/	OST	
/olt/		OLT

/ly/	LY	
/ed/	ED	

/alt/	ALT	
/ald/		ALD
/all/	ALL	
/alm/		ALM

/alk/		ALK
/olk/		OLK

/wa/		WA
/wor/	WAR	
/wer/	WOR	WAR

/quah/	QUA	
/guah/		GUA
/gar/		GUAR

/ŏt/ (combination)	OT	OUGHT, AUGHT
/īt/ (combination)	IGHT, ITE	
/ood/ (combination)	OOD	OULD

Spelling & Blending Tiles

sh	ch	th	wh
gh	ph	rh	

scr	sch	spr	spl
str	squ	shr	thr
chr	nch	tch	

ae	ee	ie	oe
ue	ye		

ea	oa	oo

ai	ay	ei	ey
oi	oy	ui	uy

au	aw	eu	ew
ou	ow		

a	e	i	o	u	y
a	e	i	o	u	y
a	e	i	o	u	y
a	e	i	o	u	y
a	e	i	o	u	y

a	b	c	d	e	f
g	h	i	j	k	l
m	n	o	p	q	r
s	t	u	v	w	x
y	z				

A	B	C	D	E	F
G	H	I	J	K	L
M	N	O	P	Q	R
S	T	U	V	W	X
Y	Z				

Glossary

Accented Syllable – the syllable that is stressed when the word is pronounced. In the word **ad-VEN-ture**, **VEN** is the accented syllable. In the word **EL-e-phant**, **EL** is the accented syllable. The accent in dictionaries is indicated by an accent mark. **ad ven' ture   el' e phant** The unaccented syllable often has a schwa sound for the vowel.

Affix – an element that is added to a root or base word to change or modify the meaning of the word. Prefixes and Suffixes are both affixes. In the word, **uncooked, UN-** and **-ED** are both affixes. Affixes are "bound." This means that they cannot stand alone as a word. They must be added to a word to express their meaning.

Base Word – a word that has meaning and can stand on its own. Some people exchange the terms Root Word and Base Word. In this book, a Root Word refers to a word with the smallest unit of meaning. It does not have any prefixes or suffixes. In contrast, in this book, a Base Word is any word that may already have additional prefixes and suffixes added to it. A Base Word that has prefixes or suffixes attached may still be able to have more suffixes and prefixes added to it. For example, in the word **reforming**, **form** is the **Root** Word. **Reform** could be considered a **Base** Word, because it can stand on its own, and it can have additional suffixes, such as **-ING** added to it **(reforming)**. However, **reform** could not be considered a Root Word, because a Root Word would not have a prefix. Roots may or may not be able to stand on their own as words. In the word, **animal, ANIM** is the root, meaning "breath" or "life," but it is not a word on its own.

Blend – two or more letters that appear together frequently, but both retain their original sounds. **PL** is a blend. The **P** and **L** retain their original sounds. **SH** is a digraph, not a blend, because the **S** and **H** in **SH** make a new sound when they are together.

Breve – a marking above a vowel, indicating the vowel's short sound.

ă ĕ ĭ ŏ ŭ

Closed Syllable – syllable that has a single vowel and ends with one or more consonants. In closed syllables, the vowel usually makes a short sound. The word **bet** is a closed syllable, because the consonant **T** "closes" the syllable and causes the **E** to say its short sound. The word **be** is an open syllable. The **E** in **be**

271

says its long sound because there is no consonant closing it. In the word **beside** (be-side), the **be** is an open syllable. In the word **kitten** (kit-ten), **kit** is a closed syllable. In the word **duckling** (duck-ling), **duck** is a closed syllable. Closed syllables can be open at the beginning, as long as they are closed at the end. In the word **advent** (ad-vent), **ad** is a closed syllable.

Closed Syllable Exception – closed syllable with a vowel sound that is not short. In closed syllables, the vowel typically makes a short sound. In closed syllable exceptions, the vowel makes a long sound, or an alternate vowel sound. These are generally taught as their own phonograms. **INK**, **OLD**, and **ALK** are examples of closed syllable exceptions.

Comparative – an adjective or adverb expressing a greater quality. Comparatives end with the suffix **-ER**. **Larger** and **faster** are comparatives. In contrast, Superlatives express the greatest quality and end in **-EST**. **Largest** and **fastest** are superlatives.

Compound Word – A compound word is a word that is made up of at least two smaller words (**baseball, butterfly**). Occasionally, you can have a word that is made up of three or more words, such as **mother-in-law.**

There are three types of compound words:

Closed Compound is a compound word that consists of two or more words that are joined together to make a single word (**playground**). The Closed compound is the most common type of compound word.

Open Compound is a compound that is made up of two words that are separate but function as a single word (**ice cream**).

Hyphenated Compound is a compound word that is made up of two or more words that are joined by a hyphen (**part-time**).

Consonant – A consonant is any letter of the alphabet that is not a vowel. It is a speech sound that is characterized by a closure or obstruction in air/breath. The consonants are **b, c, d, f, g, h, j, k, l, m, n p, q, r, s, t, v, w, x, y,** and **z**. **Y** is a consonant when it is found at the beginning of a word and makes the sound **/y/** in **yam**. **Y** is vowel when it says **/ī/** in **fly**, **/ē/** in **bunny**, **/ī/** in **type** or **/ĭ/** in **gym**.

Consonant Digraph – two consonants that make one consonant sound **(SH, CH)**. Blends **(BL, CR)** make two different sounds, but digraphs make only one sound.

Derivational and Inflectional Suffixes – Suffixes are considered either inflectional or derivational. Inflectional Suffixes retain more of the original meaning of the root word than derivations suffixes do. Linguists disagree widely on the differentiation between inflectional and derivational. In general, inflectional suffixes change the verb tense (**-ed, -ing**), indicate number/plural (**-s, -es**), show possession (**'s** in Meghan**'s** bike), and show comparison (**-er, -est**) Derivational suffixes are used to make/derive new words. They change the base word in a more significant way, most often changing the word from one grammar class to another. For example, **kind** (adjective) becomes **kindness** (noun), **hard** (adjective) becomes **harden** (verb).

Digraph – a combination of two letters that represent one sound. **CH** is a consonant digraph and **AI** is a vowel digraph.

Diphthong- a combination of two vowels, in which both vowel sounds are heard, but one vowel sound glides into the other. Those two vowel sounds are found within only one syllable. Experts disagree on the number of diphthongs, but the most common are, **OI, OY, OU,** and **OW.**

End Blend - a blend that appears primarily at the end of a root word. **CT (act), LP (help), NT (ant),** and **SK (brisk)** are all examples of end blends. Suffixes may be added to end blends, so it's important to note that end blends are at the end of root words, not necessarily the end of the word itself: **briskly, helpful, acting**.

Grapheme – the smallest written symbol of a phoneme. The term phoneme refers to the sound, whereas the term grapheme refers to the written letters. A grapheme can be only one letter **(T)**, or multiple letters **(OUGH)**. The grapheme **SH** symbolizes the phoneme **/sh/** at the beginning of the word *ship*.

Letter Team - any two or more letters that appear frequently together in words. Letter Team is a simplified way to say phonogram, digraph, blend, etc.

Long Vowel – All vowels **(A,E,I,O,U)** have at least two sounds, a short sound, and a long sound. Some vowels have other sounds, as well. The Long Sound is usually identical to the name of the vowel. For example, Long **/ā/** says the name **A**, as in the word **bake**. Long **/ō/** says the name **O**, as in **bone**. Long **U** is the only vowel with two long sounds. The first is pronounced **/yoo/**, like the name of **U**, as in the word **fuse**. The second is **/oo/**, as in the word **tune**. Long vowels are marked by the macron, which looks like a line over the vowel. **ā ē ī ō ū**

Macron - a marking above a vowel, indicating the vowel's long sound.

ā ē ī ō ū

Morpheme – the smallest unit of meaning in a word. Root words can be morphemes, and prefixes and suffixes can also be morphemes. In the word rewrite, **RE** is a morpheme that means "to do again." **WRITE** is a morpheme that means "write." In the word **writer**, **WRITE** is a morpheme that means "write", and ER is a morpheme that means "one who."

Open Syllable – a syllable that ends with a vowel and no consonant. In an open syllable, the vowel usually makes the long vowel sound. In closed syllables, the vowel usually makes a short sound. The word **bet** has a closed syllable, because the consonant **T** "closes" the syllable and causes the **E** to say its short sound. The word **be** is an open syllable. The **E** in **be** says its long sound because there is no consonant closing the syllable. In the word **beside** (be-side), **be** is an open syllable. In the word **kitten** (kit-ten), **kit** is a closed syllable. In the word **duckling** (duck-ling), **duck** is a closed syllable. Closed syllables can be open at the beginning. In the word **advent** (ad-vent), **ad** is still a closed syllable, because it is closed at the end.

Orthographic Mapping – Orthographic mapping is the process of storing printed words into long term memory. It involves seeing a word, breaking the word into letters or letter groups, translating those letters into sounds, and storing the word as a sequence of sounds (and possibly visual images) in the brain. The process or orthographic mapping requires phonemic awareness, understanding of letter/sound relationships and using the phonological long-term memory. Students with dyslexia struggle to map words into long-term memory because of a phonological-core deficit.

Phoneme – A phoneme is the smallest unit of sound in a language. /p/ and /sh/ are both phonemes. The word **boat** has four letters, but it only has three phonemes - /b/, /oa/, /t/.

Phonemic Awareness – awareness of the smallest individual sounds in a word. The terms Phonemic Awareness and Phonological Awareness are often used interchangeably in the field of education. However, phonological awareness is a broader term that refers to a general understanding that words are made up of sounds, whereas phonemic awareness focuses on the individual phonemes (sounds) in a word.

Phonological Awareness – awareness that words are made up of sounds. The terms Phonemic Awareness and Phonological Awareness are often used interchangeably in the field of education. However, phonological awareness is a broader term that refers to a general understanding that words are made up of sounds, whereas phonemic awareness focuses on the individual phonemes (sounds) in a word. Phonological awareness can cover phonemes, but it can also cover syllables, onset & rimes, etc.

Phonogram – A phonogram is a combination of a phoneme (smallest unit of sound) and a grapheme (smallest written unit). Examples of phonograms are **T, SH, WOR,** and **IGH.**

Prefix – A prefix is added on to the beginning of a base word to change the meaning of that word. Examples of prefixes include **UN-** in the word **unable** and **PRE-** in the word **prewash.**

R-Controlled – An **R**-controlled syllable has a vowel sound that is changed/influenced by the **R**. The **R**-controlled vowels are **AR, ER, IR, OR** and **UR**. Some educators would also include three-letter combinations such as **EAR** and **OAR** to be **R**-controlled.

Root - a word or word part with the smallest unit of meaning. A root word is the most basic form of a word, before prefixes and suffixes are added to it. The terms Root Word and Base Word are frequently used interchangeably in the field of education. In this book, a Base Word may already have a suffix or prefix attached, but the Base Word may still be able to have more suffixes and prefixes added to it, whereas a root word does not have any suffixes or prefixes attached. It is the most basic form of the word. For example, in the word **unzipped, zip** is the root word. **Unzip** could be considered a base word, because it can stand on its own, and it can have a suffix (**-ED**) added to it. However, **unzip** could not be considered a root word, because a root word would not have a prefix. Roots may or may not be able to stand on their own as words. In the word, animal, **ANIM** is the root, meaning "breath" or "life," but it is not a root word by itself.

Schwa – a vowel sound that makes an indistinct vowel sound, or no vowel sound at all. The schwa sound is usually found in an unaccented syllable. The sound of the schwa is close to a short /ŭ/ sound, or sometimes a short I / ĭ / sound, depending on dialect. The schwa sound can be represented by any vowel. The symbol for schwa is "ə" Examples are: **a**bove, pres**e**nt, wiz**a**rd, bott**o**m.

Self-Teaching hypothesis – hypothesis that proposes that children who have proficiency in phonemic awareness and phonic decoding teach themselves to read new words, resulting in a much larger reading vocabulary than could be achieved by learning sight words as whole words. For more information on the Self-Teaching hypothesis, see the research of David Share and Linnea C. Ehri.

Short Vowel – a vowel sound that is cut off, or shortened, by a consonant sound. The short vowels are /ă/ in bat, /ĕ/ in bed, / ĭ / in clip, /ŏ/ in hot, and /ŭ/ in bug.

Silent letter – A silent letter does not have any sound. Silent letters can exist on their own, such as the **H** in the word **herb**, or they can be a part of a letter team, such as the **L** in **OLK** (**yolk**). Silent letters may vary by dialect.

Suffix – an affix that is added on to the end of a root word. Suffixes change the meaning of a word, usually with a change in grammar. For example, in the word **goodness**, the suffix **-NESS** changes the word **good** from an adjective to **goodness**, which is a noun. In **runner**, **-ER** changes the base word from **run**, which is a verb, to **runner**, which is a noun.

Superlative – an adjective or adverb expressing the highest quality. Superlatives end in the suffix **-EST**. **Largest** and **Fastest** are superlatives. In contrast, Comparatives compare and express only a greater quality. Comparatives end in **-ER**. **Larger** and **faster** are comparatives.

Syllable – an uninterrupted unit of speech that has one vowel sound. A syllable can be an entire word, or a part of a word. Examples of words divided into syllables are: **cat, ba-by, ad-vent-ure, cel-e-bra-tion, op-por-tu-ni-ty.** The six syllable types are **Closed, CLE, Open, Vowel Team, VCE,** and **R-Controlled.** Some teachers divide the vowel team syllables into digraphs & dipthongs, making seven syllable types. The word **CLOVER** is a nice way of remembering all of the syllable types. (**C**-closed, **L**-Cle, **O**-open, **V**-vowel team, **E**-VCE, **R**-R controlled)

Trigraph – a combination of a digraph and a third letter **(SHR, CHR).** Trigraphs are sometimes called Digraph Blends.

Unaccented Syllables – all the syllables of a word that are not accented. Vowels in unaccented syllables often express a schwa sound.

Unvoiced (voiceless) - phoneme (speech sound) that uses no vocal cords to produce its sound. All vowels are voiced, so only consonants can be unvoiced. The unvoiced consonant sounds are **/f, h, k, p, s, t, ch, sh/.** **TH** has both a voiced and unvoiced sound. **TH** in **thing** is unvoiced and **TH** in **this** is voiced.

VCE – **VCE** is a syllable pattern. In a **VCE** syllable, the silent **E** at the end of a word causes the preceding vowel to say its long sound. The words **bake, poke,** and meme are all **VCE** words.

Voiced – phoneme (speech sound) that uses vocal cords to produce its sound. All vowels are voiced. The consonant sounds that are voiced are **/b, d, g, j, l, m, n, r, v, w, y, z, ng, zh/.** **TH** has both a voiced and unvoiced sound. **TH** in **thing** is unvoiced and **TH** in **this** is voiced.

Voiceless – See Unvoiced.

Vowel – a sound in which the air is not restricted. The mouth stays open when saying any vowel sound. The vowels are **A,E,I,O,U**, and sometimes **Y.** There are also many vowel teams, such as **AI, EA, OO,** etc.

Vowel Digraph – a combination of two vowels that make one sound. **(AI, EE)**

Vowel Team – a simplified way to say vowel digraph, diphthong, or any other vowel combination.

Bibliography & Resources

for Dyslexia, Phonics, and Word Study

American Heritage Children's Dictionary (2019). Houghton Mifflin Harcourt Publishing Company.

Arredondo, Valerie. (2019). *Orton-Gillingham Word List Dictionary Volume 1, 2 and 3*. Campbell Curriculum.

Ayers, Donald M. (1986). *English Words from Latin and Greek Elements*. University of Arizona Press.

Ayto, John. (2011). *Dictionary of Word Origins*. Arcade Publishing.

Barton Reading & Spelling System. www.bartonreading.com

Bauer, Laurie, et al. (2015). *The Oxford Reference Guide to English Morphology*. Oxford University Press.

Berninger, Virginia. (2016). *Teaching Students with Dyslexia, Dysgraphia, OWL, LD and Dyscalculia*. Paul H. Brookes Publishing Co.

Birsh, Judith. (2011). *Multisensory Teaching of Basic Language Skills*. Paul H. Brookes Publishing Company.

Bishop, Margaret. (1986). *The ABC's and All Their Tricks: The Complete Reference Book of Phonics and Spelling*. Mott Media.

Blevins, Wiley. (2017). *Teaching Phonics & Word Study*. Scholastic.

Carver, Lin & Pantoja, Lauren. (2009). *Teaching Syllable Patterns*. Capstone Publishing, Inc

Dyslexia Training Institute. www.dyslexiatraininginstitute.org

Eide, Brock & Eide, Fernette. (2011). *The Dyslexic Advantage*. Plume.

Eide, Denise. (2012). *Uncovering the Logic of English*. Pedia Learning, Inc.

Fox, Barbara. (2014). *Phonics and Word Study for the Teacher of Reading*. Pearson.

Freeman, David & Freeman, Yvonne. *Essential Linguistics*. Heinemann.

Fulford, John. (2012). *The Complete Guide to English Spelling Rules*. Astoria Press.

Galaburda, Albert, et al. (2018). *Dyslexia and Neuroscience*. Paul H. Brookes Publishing Co.

Ganske, Kathy, (2014). *Word Journeys*. Guilford Press.

Ganske, Kathy. (2008). *Mindful of Words*. Guilford Press.

Geffner, Donna. (2019). *Auditory Processing Disorders: Assessment, Management, and Treatment*. Plural Publishing.

Gillingham, Anna & Stillman, Bessie. *The Gillingham Manual*. Educators Publishing Service.

Haspelmath, Martin and Sims, Andrea. (2002). *Understanding Morphology (Understanding Language Series)*. Routledge.

Henry, Marcia. (2010). *Unlocking Literacy: Effective Decoding & Spelling Instruction*. Paul H. Brookes Publishing Co.

Henry, Marcia. (2010). Words: *Integrated Decoding and Spelling Instruction Based on Word Origin and Word Structure*. Pro-Ed.

Institute for Multi-Sensory Education. www.orton-gillingham.com

International Dyslexia Association. www.dyslexiaida.org

Johnson, Kristin and Bayrd, Polly. (2010). *Megawords* (series). *Educators Publishing Service*.

Honig, Bill & Diamond, Linda. (2019). *Teaching Reading Sourcebook* (Core Literacy Library). Academic Therapy Publications; Third edition.

Kilpatrick, David, et al. (2019). *Reading Development and Difficulties: Bridging the Gap Between Research and Practice*.

Kilpatrick, David. (2016). *Equipped for Reading Success*. Casey & Kirsch Publishers.

Kilpatrick, David. (2015). *Essentials of Assessing, Preventing, and Overcoming Reading Difficulties*. John Wiley & Sons, Inc.

Leu, Donald & Kinzer, Charles. (2017). *Phonics, Phonemic Awareness, and Word Analysis*. Pearson Education, Inc.

Lewis, Norman. (2014). Word Power Made Easy. Anchor Press.

Mather, Nancy. (2009). Writing Assessment and Instruction for Students with Learning Disabilities. Jossey-Bass (Wiley).

Minkova, Donka (2004). "Philology, linguistics, and the history of /hw/~/w/". In Anne Curzan; Kimberly Emmons (eds.). Studies in the History of the English language II: Unfolding Conversations.

Mather, Nancy. (2012). *Essentials of Dyslexia Assessment and Intervention*. John Wiley & Sons, Inc.

Moats, Louisa Cook. (2010). *Speech to Print: Language Essentials for Teachers*. Paul H. Brookes Publishing Co.

Moats, Louisa & Toman, Carol. *LETRS* training program for teachers.

Neil Ramsden Word Searcher. www.neilramsden.co.uk

O'Connor, Rollanda E. (2020). *Teaching Word Recognition*. The Guildord Press.

Online Etymology Dictionary. www.etymonline.com

Orton Gillingham Online Academy. www.ortongillinghamonlinetutor.com

Reid, Gavin & Guise, Jennie. (2017). *The Dyslexia Assessment*. Bloomsbury.

Rippel, Marie. All About Learning curriculum. www.allaboutlearningpress.com

Rome, Paula & Osman, Jean. (2000). *Advanced Language Tool Kit*. Educators Publishing Services.

Rome, Paula & Osman, Jean. (2004). *Language Tool Kit*. Educators Publishing Services.

Ruding, Joanne. (2017). *Spelling Rules Workbook*. How to Spell Publishing.

Shaywitz, Sally. (2003). *Overcoming Dyslexia*. Vintage Books.

The Yale Center for Dyslexia & Creativity. www.dyslexia.yale.edu

Venezky, Richard. (1999). *The American Way of Spelling: The Structure and Origins of American English Orthography*. Guilford Press.

Wilson Reading System. www.wilsonlanguage.com

Zafarris, Jess. (2020). *Once Upon a Word: A Word-Origin Dictionary*. Rockridge Press.

Printed in Great Britain
by Amazon